# Beat IR35

## The ultimate guide to IR35 for contractors, agencies and clients

# Praise for Chaplin's other work

*I have been an independent contractor with my own limited company for 6 months and I am finding this book absolutely indispensable. It was a great checklist for start-up activities and for someone who has not yet taken the leap, it is a great support resource. There are chapters on marketing oneself to contracts and IR35, as well as lots of advice on how to comply with HMRC processes with as little stress as possible.*

PigPig's Amazon review (Contractors' Handbook: The Expert Guide for UK Contractors and Freelancers Ed 2)

*There is some great stuff in here even if you are already contracting. Advice on the lurking monster that is IR35 is always welcome, and sound advice is offered on this topic in this book.*

A. Gothorp's Amazon review (Contractors' Handbook: The Expert Guide for UK Contractors and Freelancers Ed 1)

*This book pretty much matched exactly what I was looking for and it was well worth investing the time required to read it properly. There are sections about the various different options for starting up a company, and contract law. There's also a suitably massive section about IR35. It was extremely useful, and will probably continue to be useful as I start to get used to life as a contractor.*

Number Six's Amazon review (Contractors' Handbook: The Expert Guide for UK Contractors and Freelancers Ed 1)

*The Contractors Handbook has encouraged me to start doing a lot of the stuff that I ought to have been doing anyway, like keeping contract files in case HMRC ever wants to look into my IR35 status. Buy the Contractors' Handbook and it will probably save you making costly mistakes.*

*Greatly recommended.*

IT Jane's Amazon review (Contractors' Handbook: The Expert Guide for UK Contractors and Freelancers Ed 1)


*THE Bible for anyone wanting to start their own limited company and venture into the contracting world.*

A. Chilcott's Amazon review (Contractors' Handbook: The Expert Guide for UK Contractors and Freelancers Ed 1)

By the same author:

Contractors' Handbook: The Expert Guide for UK
Contractors and Freelancers
Second edition

*For further information about other publications from Byte-Vision, please contact:*

Marketing Department

IR35 Testing

An imprint of Byte-Vision Ltd

67 Colney Lane

Norwich

NR4 7RG

# Beat IR35

The ultimate guide to IR35 for contractors, agencies and clients

Dave Chaplin

Copyright © 2017 IR35 Testing

First published in 2017 by IR35 Testing

IR35 Testing

An imprint of Byte-Vision Ltd

67 Colney Lane

Norwich

NR4 7RG

British Library Cataloguing in Publication Data:

ISBN 978-152031 7496

Dedicated the UK's contractors and freelancers, for all of your hard work.

Please note: all content is believed to be correct at time of writing (January 2017), and is based on our current understanding of the law and HMRC practice. We have attempted to indicate where legislation has not been finalised.

# Preface

More than a decade and a half on from the introduction of IR35 and HMRC is still very much active in its pursuit of 'disguised employees'. In October 2016 our team at ContractorCalculator.co.uk broke the news that more than 100 BBC presenters operating through their own limited companies had been targeted in a large scale IR35 clampdown by the taxman.

It remains a difficult hurdle that the UK's contractors and freelancers constantly have to adapt to overcome, and it looks as if it's only going to get tougher as HMRC continues its misguided fight against tax avoidance. The signs are ominous. Following the BBC revelation – the most high profile crackdown in IR35's history – the much maligned public sector reforms continued to progress towards implementation. IR35 is arguably more of a threat than ever before.

Nonetheless, the UK contract sector continues to thrive, and is frequently acknowledged for its contribution to the economy. Whether it's for providing clients across a wide range of sectors with the skills and expertise necessary to meet project objectives - skills that they often can't afford to source in-house – or for playing a critical role in driving the UK out of recession following the 2008/09 financial crisis, contractors have gained recognition as an indispensable division of the labour market.

An increasing number of contractors and clients alike are realising the mutual benefits of flexible working. Research from the Association of Independent Professionals and the Self Employed (IPSE) points towards continued strong growth in the contractor sector, with estimates suggesting that there were 1.91 million contractors and freelancers working in the UK in 2015.

The contribution of the flexible workforce to the UK labour market hasn't gone unnoticed by the Government either. In July 2015 former PM David Cameron commissioned a review examining the challenges faced by the self-employed, led by Julie Deane OBE. In October 2016 PM Theresa May launched a review into employment practices to help support the growing number of workers striking out on their own.

In spite of this, HMRC repeatedly rears its ugly head, and policy impacting contractors continues to contradict the otherwise positive messages coming from Westminster. The IR35 Forum came along in 2012, adding a further layer of complication for limited company contractors to deal with in the form of the business entity tests. These tests were deemed not fit for purpose and were subsequently scrapped in April 2015. However, the Government continues to press ahead with further legislation, with its public sector reforms of IR35 in April 2017.

There is a very real possibility that the public sector rules will be extended into the private sector, so contractors and engagers may need to prepare themselves for the most significant change to IR35 since its introduction in April 2000.

This continued attack on contractors is the reason why we have published Beat IR35. One of the biggest risks to your IR35 status is actually yourself. Contractors that do not take pre-emptive action to combat any future investigation are the ones more likely to fail, facing huge tax bills and penalties. But that needn't be a concern because everything you need to know about the IR35 legislation and how to overcome it is right here.

At ContractorCalculator.co.uk we have been following IR35 since the legislation's inception. Throughout this time, we have developed products and guides to help contractors navigate the legislation and minimise their risk, and have consulted extensively with the Treasury and HMRC on IR35 matters.

Pooling all this expertise, along with knowledge of employment case law upon which IR35 is based, into this book means Beat IR35 is the all-encompassing guide you need to ensure you remain compliant. Whether you're a contractor, client or agency, providing you do everything by the book, there is very little chance that the taxman will come knocking.

Dave Chaplin
CEO ContractorCalculator,
January 2017

# 1

# Why IR35 matters to you

## 1.1 What is IR35?

IR35 is tax legislation aimed at countering tax avoidance, and specifically targets limited company contractors. Being caught by IR35 could see you lose out on tens of thousands of pounds worth of contracting income per year to the taxman. As a result, a comprehensive understanding of IR35 and how to avoid the legislation has become essential for all contractors.

IR35 focuses on contractors who, according to employment law, would be an employee of the client if they did not work through an intermediary such as a limited company, which is the most common vehicle contractors use to supply their services.

As a limited company contractor, you are entitled to pay less tax than an employee, who will have income tax and NICs (National Insurance contributions) deducted from their earnings via Pay As You Earn (PAYE). However, at the same time you do not receive the employment rights available to employees, such as holiday and sick pay and enrolment into company pension schemes. Neither do you have the same job security.

Contractors are happy to accept this as a fair exchange, as their contracting earnings are often greater than what they would earn as an equivalent employee. However, HMRC's view that contractors caught by IR35 should be taxed as employees without receiving the equivalent rights has been a continuing source of contention.

The bad news is that employment status isn't a choice you make. It is defined in law, and can be overridden by the taxman. If HMRC believes the terms of your work as a contractor make you a 'disguised employee', you could receive the equivalent tax treatment that could result in a reduction of up to 20% of your take-home pay after taxes.

This is why it's essential that you're well equipped to ensure IR35 doesn't affect your earnings.

Fortunately, with this book, you have everything you need to beat IR35.

## What is IR35 for?

The idea behind IR35 is to stop firms hiring employees via service companies and therefore avoiding the overheads of employment such as costly tax and employment benefits. It's also to stop firms converting employees to contractors overnight to achieve the same goals – the so called "Friday-to-Monday" situation.

In other words, it's the Treasury's and HMRC's way of making sure people pay the tax they're supposed to. In their view 'disguised employees' are not genuine contractors providing business-to-business services, and should therefore be employed, resulting in more tax being paid.

In practice IR35 requires HMRC to prove on a case-by-case basis that a contractor under investigation is not really a small business, but is actually an employee. This means, employment status case law must be used to determine the correct status. That's why you will see frequent references to employment law, 'status tests', 'status enquiries' and 'tests of employment' in this book and other writings about IR35.

There are many critics of the basic legislation itself. Most conclude that IR35 is unworkable. But, unworkable or not, it is law and HMRC has to apply it, and apply it rigorously, to meet its revenue-collection targets.

## Why should you care about IR35?

So why should you be worrying about such a complex piece of tax and employment legislation?

Answer: Because it could cost you thousands of pounds every year if you don't. Being found inside IR35 could result in a serious decrease in your income – in fact it could cause up to a 20% reduction in your take-home pay. The fallout if HMRC challenges you and finds that you have been being non-compliant is even worse.

Whilst you are contracting via a limited company you will be at risk of HMRC conducting an IR35 review to determine whether your contracts are covered by the legislation. It doesn't stop there. You might have stopped contracting, but any historic contracts can still be challenged leaving you liable for tax you should have paid from up to six years ago.

If HMRC suspects fraud at any point during an investigation, it can trace your contracting career as far back as 20 years, so remaining IR35-compliant throughout your career is essential. Fortunately, providing you diligently follow the guidance set out in this book, you can minimise your risk of ever having a run in with the taxman.

If not, you could find yourself suffering a massive tax hit running into tens of thousands of pounds. In the Special Commissioners case Dragonfly Consulting v HMRC [2008] contractor John Bessell was faced with a tax bill for £99,000 after the judge ruled that his contract was caught by IR35.

**How is IR35 status determined?**

The taxman claims that IR35 was introduced to make sure that 'people who do the same job in the same manner pay broadly similar amounts of income tax and National Insurance'. However, this is entirely misguided in the eyes of the law, because the actual laws regarding employment status are more concerned with how the engagement works in practice, not what job is actually done.

Whether a contract is within IR35 or not is not a black and white decision. The legislation is underpinned by complex employment case law dating back over several decades. IR35 is subjective and can only be determined on a case-by-case basis. In truth, the only way you will ever know your IR35 status for certain is by going to tax tribunal, such is the complexity of the legislation.

The three key factors that need to be considered when determining IR35 are:

- Personal service/substitution – has the client hired your company or you personally? Are you able to provide a substitute to carry out the work?
- Control – does the client control you?
- Mutuality of obligation (MOO) – are you obliged to accept work offered, and is the client obliged to offer you work?

These are known as the 'tests of employment' and they underpin all UK employment status cases. In addition to these, there are further, smaller factors that will also influence a decision on IR35. These include:

- Financial risk – do you risk your own money and is there opportunity for you to gain financially through sound management?
- Part and parcel – are you a 'fixture' of the client's organisation, similar to an employee?
- Provision of equipment – do you use your own equipment to do the job?

The factors impacting your IR35 status are explained in greater detail in chapter 5.

**Public and private sector differences**

When IR35 was introduced in 2000 all contractors were:

- Responsible for determining their own IR35 status
- Liable for any unpaid taxes and penalties, should IR35 investigate and rule against them

This has been the case for contractors in both the public and private sectors since April 2000. However, from April 2017, public sector clients are to assume responsibility for determining each contractor's IR35 status.

Where there is an agency in the contractor supply chain, as there will be in most cases, they will be responsible for calculating, reporting and paying tax on behalf of the contractor where the client determines that the contractor is caught by IR35. If there is no agency present, the responsibility rests with the client.

HMRC has yet to confirm who will be liable for backdated tax, penalties and interest if a client judges a contractor to be outside IR35 and it is subsequently proven that they are inside. However, it is expected that the liability will fall with either the client or the agency. If it is proven that the contractor used fraudulent documentation to prove their outside status to the client, the contractor is liable.

For a more comprehensive overview of the reforms and their anticipated impact on the contractor supply chain, see chapters 4 and 6.

**How do IR35 investigations work?**

Anyone trading outside the scope of IR35 may still be investigated by HMRC at a later date. This could mean the contractor or the client or agency owing a significant sum in unpaid back taxes, interest and penalties, depending on whether it is a public or private sector engagement. Penalties can be more severe if HMRC can prove that IR35 rules have been deliberately ignored.

This is complicated, and it is not yet known how the bill for back taxes will be shared between those concerned in the public sector. Investigations, and the penalties they can lead to aren't small. They are meant as a deterrent.

As a contractor you can simply take the time to understand IR35, how it works and its potential impact on you and your business. With what you'll learn from this book, if you take some straightforward, sensible precautions, you should have no problem understanding the position, meaning you'll pay no more tax than you need to.

The best way to protect yourself from an HMRC investigation is to conduct your due diligence for each and every contract you agree to. In this book we explain the necessary procedure. We suggest you begin by having your contract evaluated for free using the online tool ir35testing.co.uk. For further expert guidance on minimising your risk of being caught by IR35, go to chapter 8 of this book.

**When does IR35 not apply?**

IR35 only applies to contractors who operate via limited companies.

IR35 does not apply to:

- Umbrella company workers
- Sole traders
- Offshore payment solutions – although due diligence is required

If you work through an umbrella company, you are already technically an employee subject to full PAYE and NICs, so you are not affected.

Similarly, as a sole trader you pay income tax and NICs on your profits, so IR35 does not apply. If you have chosen to trade via an offshore solution, you should check with your scheme provider about your employment status and whether IR35 applies.

**How many contractors get caught by IR35?**

IR35 has traditionally suffered from ineffective enforcement and has consistently struggled to hit its anticipated tax yield, but developments in 2016 show that HMRC is making big moves to clamp down on those it suspects to be flaunting the rules.

The public sector reform is the biggest thing to happen to IR35 since its inception, and marks a signal of intent from HMRC, which is evidently ramping up its efforts. With a similar private sector rollout expected, carrying out due diligence to ensure contracts remain outside IR35 becomes all the more important.

There is an estimated population of around 400,000 contractors operating through limited companies in the UK at any one time. HMRC's records show that during the first decade that IR35 was in force, between 2,000 and 29,000 contractors self-certified themselves as within IR35 each year. However, this only tells part of the story.

Unofficial statistics show that thousands of cases never made the official list because the contractors concerned, and their professional advisers, shut down the initial IR35 investigation immediately. This was because they had a watertight case for being outside IR35 based on the strategies described in this book. The evidence was sent to HMRC by the contractor's IR35 professional advisers on day one and that meant any further IR35 investigation was doomed to failure from the outset.

In addition to this, the news, broken by this book's publisher ContractorCalculator in October 2016 that the taxman opened investigations into the tax affairs of more than 100

BBC broadcasters operating through limited companies provides proof that HMRC is still very much active on the IR35 front, so contractors need to be on guard.

## How contractors should deal with IR35

HMRC isn't one to back down, and is known to fight many cases even when it loses. Investigations are still very prevalent, although few make it to tribunal as they are often settled beforehand. Precautions do need to be taken though. And by following the measures highlighted in this book you should avoid ever having to go face to face with the taxman in court.

Even if you win, the cost and hassle of a long investigation is not good. You want to make sure you're insured and also well prepared so you can cut short any investigation that may arise. That means making a pre-emptive defence. The cost of an investigation defence isn't cheap, and even if you are confident about your status you should get tax investigation insurance, which will cost circa £100-£150.

Defending your IR35 status is very much a pre-emptive strategy. HMRC's inspectors are looking for easy targets – don't be one. With forethought and correct planning, you too can ensure you remain outside IR35 throughout your contracting career. With this book you have everything you need to beat IR35.

# 1.2 A brief history of IR35

IR35 - 'Intermediaries Legislation' - was first announced in the Pre-Budget speech of 1999 by then Chancellor Gordon Brown, and adopted as part of the Finance Act for April 2000.

The "IR" part stems from the original Inland Revenue (now called HMRC) and the "35" comes from the number of the press release in which it was announced. The entire industry refers to it as "IR35".

IR35 key facts:

- Introduced to tackle what the Treasury referred to as 'disguised employment'
- The legislation survived a judicial review of its legality in 2001
- HMRC believes the deterrent effect of IR35 generates £550m for the Exchequer each year
- A public scandal sparked changes known as the 'off-payroll rules', specifically targeting public sector contractors in 2012
- Public sector contractors are to be further impacted by reforms to IR35, in effect from April 2017

**Why IR35 was created**

The motivation for the Treasury was to stop firms hiring employees via service companies, allowing both parties to avoid large amounts of tax in the process. IR35 came in response to the fallout from a surge in demand for IT personnel in the 1990s, where many IT employees left their permanent positions and incorporated in order to earn more money. Soon enough, the majority of the UK IT workforce were contractors. They were paid much more and paid more tax overall, but HMRC didn't see it that way.

Some firms, to retain staff allowed them to leave on a Friday to return on a Monday doing the same thing, but as a contractor. HMRC leapt on the relatively rare Friday-to-Monday scenario, using it to justify the new rules, which it believed would combat tax avoidance.

**HMRC sought to protect tax revenues**

The Treasury's view in 1999 was that a large number of contractors should have been treated as employees on the payroll of the end client. If the intermediary, such as the limited company were removed, the Treasury argued, a large number of these workers would be 'disguised employees' who should therefore be hired as employees. This means being included on the payroll and having income tax and NICs deducted at source each month.

## IR35 sent shock waves through contracting industry

From its inception, IR35 sent shock waves through the contracting sector, and opposition to the legislation was fierce. Shortly after the proposals were announced the Professional Contractors Group (PCG), now the Association of Independent Professionals and the Self Employed (IPSE), was formed to combat the legislation.

PCG took HMRC to judicial review over the legality of IR35 in March 2001, arguing that it was a breach of both human rights and European law. These arguments were dismissed by the judge who ruled in favour of HMRC.

In March 2011, a report by the Office of Tax Simplification (OTS), a body introduced by the Chancellor to simplify the UK's tax code, recommended that either IR35 be suspended, or its administration be improved.

## IR35 Forum

But the Chancellor of the day George Osborne chose the 'better administration' route, and in April 2011 appointed a body called the IR35 Forum to identify how this could be done. The Forum's membership includes relevant HMRC department heads and technical staff, and a range of tax and accounting professionals, recruitment and contracting sector representatives, including IPSE.

## Scandal sparks public sector witch-hunt

In 2012, the revelation that then Student Loans Company chief executive Ed Lester was trading as a limited company interim management contractor prompted a Government and media driven witch-hunt aimed at forcing a change to the limited company trading structure.

The Treasury proceeded to carry out a review into Government use of 'off-payroll workers' in the public sector, which in turn led to the introduction of the 'off-payroll rules' in September 2012. These stipulated that any public sector client hiring a contractor for more than six months or earning £220 or more a day must ensure that their tax affairs are in order or place them on their payroll. A study concluded that 90% of them were found to have had their tax affairs in order.

**The failed Business Entity Tests (BETs)**

The IR35 Forum spent 12 months working on a new framework to 'better administer' IR35 that was released in May 2012 to much criticism, not only by advisers, tax professionals and contractor service providers, but also by many non-HMRC members of the Forum.

The purpose of the business entity tests (BETs) was to establish a risk factor of being caught by IR35. Non-HMRC representatives of the IR35 Forum pushed for the entry level test to be used as a filter mechanism to help quickly identify genuine contractors. However, HMRC opted to use its own scoring mechanism, meaning contractors were doomed to fail the test. Dave Chaplin, CEO of ContractorCalculator, wasn't joking when he said the test was the same as asking: "Does your first name begin with a letter between A and Z? Yes, then there is a good chance you might be caught."

Following its release in May 2012, many contractor clients incorrectly identified the BETs as an IR35 status test. This was in spite of the fact that the BETs had no basis in the employment status case law that underpins IR35 legislation. In October 2014 HMRC accepted that the BETs did not work and announced their withdrawal effective from 6 April 2015.

## IR35 reviewed by House of Lords Committee

HMRC struggled to effectively enforce IR35, and the legislation was scrutinised by a House of Lords committee on PSCs in November 2013. It was revealed following a written request by a Member of Parliament that HMRC's tax yield from IR35 for 2013-14 amounted to just £430,000, £270,000 less than the £700,000 estimated annual cost of administering the legislation.

HMRC argued that the deterrent effect of IR35 generated £550m for the Exchequer in the same year, yet was unable to substantiate its claim. The House of Lords committee's scathing review of what it described as "especially cumbersome" legislation likely led to the more vigilant enforcement that we see today, epitomised by the game-changing public sector reforms.

## March 2016 budget

The Chancellor used the March 2016 Budget to announce the biggest change to IR35 since its inception, with the proposed public sector IR35 reforms. The changes, which proposed shifting the IR35 compliance burden and associated tax liability from public sector contractors over to their clients and agencies, were then further outlined in a consultation released in May 2016. Despite an outcry from the contract sector, the Government used the November 2016 Autumn Statement to confirm the reforms would go ahead and would be implemented from April 2017. Draft legislation was published in December 2016.

## BBC public sector witch-hunt

In October 2016, ContractorCalculator broke the news that more than 100 BBC presenters operating through limited companies had been targeted as part of a large scale IR35 clampdown by HMRC. It was also revealed that HMRC intended to initiate IR35 proceedings in relation to broadcasters engaged by other organisations, significantly widening the scope of its crackdown, whilst sending a warning out to the contract sector that the taxman meant business.

# 1.3 Public sector IR35 reforms – from April 2017

The public sector IR35 reforms mark the most significant event in the history of the legislation since its inception, and bring changes impacting on the whole of the contractor supply chain. The most notable changes, to be implemented in April 2017, are:

- Responsibility for checking contractor IR35 status moves to the end client
- Agency assumes responsibility for calculating, reporting and paying tax on contractor payments where the contractor is deemed to be inside IR35
- If there is no agency in the supply chain, the client taxes the contractor

HMRC is yet to confirm who will be liable for backdated tax, penalties and interest when an incorrect IR35 judgement is made, though it is expected to be either the client or the agency. It is believed that only where a contractor is found to have provided fraudulent evidence to prove their IR35 status will they be liable.

**Public sector reforms – likely impact**

A survey of the contract sector published in August 2016 by ContractorCalculator indicated that cooperation with the new rules amongst contractors was likely to be low, whilst

HMRC's anticipated tax take looked unlikely. Key points from the study included:

- 80% of contractors said they would sooner abandon the public sector than accept an inside IR35 contract
- 59% said they would push up their contract rates to account for lost income
- This would result in a £610m rise in annual costs for hiring the same people for Government
- HMRC stands to lose £115m each year by forcing contractors into fixed term employment

Administration of the scheme also looks to prove costly, not only for public sector clients and agencies, but also for the taxman. HMRC has anticipated that the regime will cost £500,000 for its implementation. However, experts speaking at a July 2016 IPSE roundtable meeting pointed out that with what the taxman estimates to be 26,000 public sector contractors requiring testing, the burden on HMRC to provide support would be immense. This now means that IR35 is a problem for more than just contractors.

**Mitigating the impact on clients and agencies**

The consequence of the reforms are significant compliance requirements upon the public sector supply chain. Most concerning for contractors, it is believed that this, accompanied by the potential financial risk makes many hirers more reluctant to offer outside IR35 contracts. This risk adverse approach can result in many legitimate public sector contractors unjustifiably taxed as employees.

Clients and agencies need to be fully aware of measures that can be taken to ensure IR35 compliance without incurring significant costs. This in turn then helps to ensure public sector contractors can continue to secure outside-IR35 contracts and only pay the necessary tax.

Fortunately, as we detail in this book, firms can make sure they follow necessary compliance procedures to ensure an outside-IR35 contract is achieved. This is simple and needn't impose any further risk upon any of the parties involved. For contractors, the first step to achieving this is testing their IR35 status online using ir35testing.co.uk. This is a free-to-use, case law-backed solution that provides an accurate assessment of the status of any particular contract. If the contract fails the test it will explain why, what you can do, and provide access to specialist providers who can help.

**No change in the private sector, for now**

If your contract is with a private sector client, it is still your responsibility to take reasonable care to make an IR35 judgement on behalf of your company. This should be based on your own due diligence and the advice you take from an IR35 and employment law specialist. However, with experts predicting that the public sector rules will also be rolled out into the private sector, all contractor clients and agencies may play a part in IR35 compliance.

For more information on the public sector reforms, guidance on all elements of contracting, and the latest updates from your industry, visit ContractorCalculator.co.uk, the UK's leading website for contractors.

# 1.4 The financial impact of IR35

If you are caught by IR35 you could suffer a reduction of up to 20% in take-home pay, the 'cash' left in your pocket after paying all your taxes and NICs. This is largely down to the fact that limited company contractors who aren't caught by IR35 aren't subject to NICs.

Instead, a contractor outside IR35 will typically pay themselves a low salary circa £8,000 per year, which is under the NICs threshold. The rest of their income is taken via dividends, paid out of the company profits after corporation tax is applied at 20%. As a result of the dividend tax hikes introduced in April 2016, the gap between what an inside-IR35 contractor and an outside-IR35 contractor earn after tax has narrowed, but it is still significant.

Limited company contractors caught by IR35 have to end up paying all their earnings out as salary, thereby paying both employees and employer's NI contributions via their limited company before receiving their take-home pay. Importantly, all the while the contractor is receiving nothing in the way of employment rights, despite paying significantly more to the taxman.

Table 1.1 shows a comparison of the tax treatment of two contractors who both made £80,000 in gross income in a year, one of whom was outside IR35 and the other inside.

|  | Limited company (inside IR35) | Limited company (outside IR35) |
|---|---|---|
| Gross income | £80,000 | £80,000 |
| Salary | £71,282 | £8,060 |
| Gross profit before tax | N/A | £71,940 |
| Employers N.I. | £8,717.53 | N/A |
| Employees N.I. | £4,758.85 | N/A |
| PAYE | £17,712.59 | N/A |
| Corporation tax | N/A | £14,388 |
| Net profit | N/A | £57,552 |
| Income tax on dividends | N/A | £9,373 |
| Income after taxes | £48,811 | £56,239 |

Table 1.1 Comparing tax paid inside and outside IR35

In this instance the contractor who is outside IR35 pays 13.2% less tax, not an insignificant sum! Depending on what your hourly or daily rate is, the impact on you of being caught by IR35 could be even greater.

As you can see from table 1.2, the financial impact of a contractor being inside IR35 is considerable. But don't fear, not all is lost, because avoiding IR35 is certainly possible if you are a genuine business and are clear about how to demonstrate your non-employee status.

| Rate per hour | Monthly take-home pay (outside IR35) | Impact of IR35 on monthly take-home pay after taxes |
|---|---|---|
| £20 | £2,073 | Decreases 16% (£342) |
| £30 | £3,090 | Decreases 18% (£579) |
| £40 | £3,920 | Decreases 18% (£716) |
| £50 | £4,663 | Decreases 17% (£792) |
| £75 | £6,519 | Decreases 15% (£1,012) |
| £100 | £7,994 | Decreases 14% (£1,162) |
| £125 | £9,784 | Decreases 14% (£1,373) |

Table 1.2 Comparing differences in tax paid and take-home pay received with an inside IR35 contract

To find out exactly how much your contracting income would suffer as a result of being caught by IR35, visit: ContractorCalculator.co.uk/ir35calculator.aspx

# 1.5 Chapter summary - key lessons for contractors, agencies and clients

## Contractors

- IR35 targets contractors who it believes would be an employee of the end client if they did not work through an intermediary such as their limited company.

- As a limited company contractor, you pay less tax than employees, although you do not qualify for any employment rights available to employees.

- HMRC frequently carries out investigations and fights many cases. The cost of a defence isn't cheap, so you are advised to take out tax investigation insurance.

## Agencies

- When IR35 was introduced in 1999, all contractors were responsible for determining their own IR35 status and paying necessary taxes and penalties, should HMRC rule against them.

- However, changes to IR35 from April 2017 mean a significant administrative burden for agencies engaging inside-IR35 public sector contractors, who assume responsibility for calculating and deducting tax from contractor pay.

- HMRC estimates that at least 26,000 public sector contractors require testing for IR35 under the new regime, meaning thousands are likely to require having taxes processed by agencies.

## Clients

- If you are a public sector client engaging contractors, changes to IR35 from April 2017 mean you are responsible for checking the IR35 status of contractors.

- Anyone trading outside the scope of IR35 can still be investigated by HMRC at a later date, which could possibly mean you owing a significant sum in unpaid back taxes, so rigid compliance is essential.

- Making sure contractors take an online IR35 test prior to beginning each contract is a cheap and efficient means of helping to determine IR35 status and conducting due diligence. To begin testing status, visit ir35testing.co.uk.

# 2

# Different models of working

## 2.1 Different models of working – why you need to understand them

Employment status isn't a choice, it's a matter of law. You may trade via a limited company, but if your working practices mirror that of an employee, the law dictates that you must be taxed the same. It's absolutely critical that you ensure you don't end up working like an employee, or else you'll find yourself handing thousands more over to the taxman each year.

Here we explain the different models of working and highlight the key differences, so you can be fully aware of what to watch out for when starting and carrying out a contract.

**Policymakers are out of touch**

Legal and policymakers' definitions of employment status no longer accurately reflect the increasing range of working arrangements used by the UK workforce. The old style definitions that applied up until the tail end of the 20th century, when most people had a career with only a few employers, don't apply to the current era of project-based work carried out by today's knowledge-based professionals. Legislation has not kept up-to-date, and it has become increasingly challenging to correctly define your employment status.

In spite of the many calls for changes to legislation, we still appear to be in deadlock. The Taylor review into employment practices was launched by the Government in November 2016, aiming to shine a light on non-traditional employment. However, with the main focus being on whether the current employment rights framework is fit for purpose, it remains to be seen whether any progress will be made in legally defining new ways of work.

**Each working model – a summary**

There are four key working models to consider. Whilst you will be engaged as a limited company contractor, the only one of the four that is affected by IR35, it's important to distinguish between each model to ensure your working practices do not begin to mirror those of any other type of worker, thus putting you at risk of IR35.

Permanent employment
- Required to perform a personal service for the employer
- Obliged to complete any task asked of them - heavily controlled.
- These working practices must be avoided at all costs by contractors

Limited company contracting
- Engaged under a contract for services – no personal service required
- Not controlled by the client
- Able to access better tax efficiency strategies than employees

Sole traders
- Self-employed, though earnings are taxed differently to limited company contractors
- Not affected by IR35 as National Insurance Contributions (NICs) are paid
- Contractors and clients need to draw clear distinction to avoid confusion

Workers
- Engaged in temporary work, though working practices don't differ too much from those of an employee
- Eligible for certain employment rights
- A limited company contractor should also avoid being judged a worker, because it's very close to the

status of an employee, and therefore a risk of being inside IR35.

## Uncertainty poses major problem for contractors

Whilst there are differences between the current models of working, there is very little certainty over what differentiates an employment relationship from a business-to-business relationship. Though definitions of employment types exist, the interpretations of policymakers, HMRC, tax law experts and employment law experts often differ, compounding the confusion.

This lack of certainty poses a problem for many limited company contractors. IR35 investigations by the taxman aren't uncommon, and contractors must diligently apply best practice to ensure their working arrangements aren't considered by HMRC to be employment relationships.

In practice, most contractors, typically highly skilled knowledge workers, operate via their own limited company and may also be employed by it. The self-employed are generally sole traders and in business on their own account. These two groups are distinct from employees and workers, who are not in business, although workers are self-employed.

## Minimising your risk of IR35

Understanding the fundamental case law rules that determine employment and self-employment and knowing what to include and avoid when negotiating a contract will put you in good stead to avoid the significant tax hit that comes with falling inside IR35.

Due diligence is vital when approaching a new contract. In chapter 8 of this book we detail the necessary steps you need to take to compliantly confirm your IR35 status, including testing each individual contract online using ir35testing.co.uk and securing an expert IR35 contract review. This way your risk of being caught by IR35 is kept to a minimum, whilst you have a strong body of evidence to back you up if HMRC ever challenges you.

# 2.2 Permanent employment

To know how to operate as a contractor you need to know what practices to avoid to ensure you don't get classed as an employee. Whilst, in practice, occasionally the work and duties carried out by a contractor may resemble that of an employee, there are usually many subtle differences. Likewise, there are several aspects of employment, such as contractual conditions and typical working practices that you need to avoid at all costs if you're a contractor.

An employment contract is a contract between an employee and employer. Whilst a contractor contract will explicitly specify certain deliverables and define due dates for completion of an assignment, an employee contract is far less stringent.

A permanent employee operates under what is known as a *contract of service*, which sets out their employment conditions, rights and general responsibilities. Both parties must abide by the contract until either the employee hands in their notice and leaves, or the employer makes them redundant or dismisses them.

**What rights are available to employees?**

The most notable differences between employment and self-employment – and key when considering the taxation of contractors as employees – are the various statutory employment rights granted to employees under employment legislation. These include:

- Statutory sick pay
- Statutory maternity/paternity leave and pay

- Paid holiday leave
- Minimum notice periods if their employment is due to end
- Protection against unfair dismissal
- Statutory redundancy pay

Employees have a specific commitment to the companies they work for and, unlike contractors, are required to perform a personal service, i.e. do the work themselves. This is critical when determining the difference between an employee and contractor, who will typically seek to include a right of substitution in a contract to demonstrate that no personal service is required. This is explained in more detail in section 5.7.

**Employees are controlled**

Possibly most important though, is control. In an employment contract, an employee is obliged to complete any task asked of them by their employer, within the remit of their job description. The explicit nature of a contractor's business-to-business contract makes it all the more important that they don't complete additional tasks asked of them after the contract has been agreed.

If a contractor is found to be performing work that deviates from the tasks highlighted in the contract, there are grounds for a strong claim that they are subject to the control of the client and are therefore subject to IR35. This is explained more comprehensively in section 5.6.

**Mutuality of obligation**

Another important distinction is that employers and employees have a 'mutuality of obligation' (MOO) to each other which is unique to the employment relationship. Basically this means: 'I am obliged to turn up for work and you, my employer, are obliged to find me work and pay me'. MOO should not apply to any working arrangement between a limited company contractor and client, and there are several steps you can take to ensure it doesn't (explained further in chapter 8).

Naturally, an employment contract provides several indicators of employment that contractors need steer well clear of. Critical IR35-determining factors such as control and MOO must be addressed in a contractor's contract. Any provision of employment rights provides damning evidence of employment status and should be avoided by contractors at all costs.

**Taxation of employees**

Permanent employees are taxed at source by their employer and use the PAYE (Pay as you earn) system. There are three taxes that are paid:
- Income tax
- National Insurance Contributions (NICs).
    - Employers NICs – paid by employers once a year on expenses and benefits given to their employees
    - Employees NICs – deducted from an employees pay check from their employer

**Temporary workers**

Some people work as temporary workers. So, for example, when working for a temp agency the person will be employed by that temp agency under an employment contract. Even if the person only works for a day, they have an employment contract for that day with all the rights that come with employment.

# 2.3 Limited company contracting

There are several ways in which a contractor can do business, although in practice most will either work via their own limited company or through an umbrella company. The former is the most popular option, as it brings with it opportunities for much great tax efficient strategies and control over their business affairs.

Here's how contractors work via limited companies:

1. The contractor sets up a limited company
2. They are a director, and often own all the company shares
3. The company employs them and pays them a small salary
4. They work for clients and the company sends out invoices and gets paid
5. The company has expenses, makes a profit, pays Corporation Tax and the money left over can be paid to the shareholder using dividends.

**No personal liability and more financial control**

Trading via a limited company means you have a trading entity that is legally separate from you. This means that your company can enter into business-to-business agreements that are separate from you as an individual. The company has the relationship with the client or agency and therefore any liability that may arise, not you personally. Employees, on the other hand, have a direct relationship with their employer. There is no intermediary.

As well as ensuring that personal and business assets are separate, a limited company is central to enjoying several benefits that attract contractors to this way of working in the first place, including:

- Greater tax efficiencies available due to running a small business
- Greater control and flexibility with regards to extracting profits/earnings

**Managing a limited company**

As a limited company contractor you will become a director and shareholder of your company. You may also opt to have spouses, family members or business colleagues as co-directors and/or shareholders, which can yield further significant and legitimate tax advantages. For more information on making legitimate tax savings by splitting dividends, visit ContractorCalculator.co.uk for a wealth of expert guide material.

You receive either some or all of your income via dividends, which can be paid out after Corporation Tax is applied to gross profits. Dividends attract income tax but at tax rates that are lower than if the money was paid out as salary. This is mainly because dividends do not attract NICs, making them the most tax-efficient means of drawing profits from a company.

Also, as long as your company is profitable, you can choose when to take dividends. This can often work to a contractor's advantage. For example, if a contractor is approaching the end of a tax year but still has some of their basic rate allowance to use up, they may wish to withdraw dividends up to just below the higher rate threshold, before the new tax year begins.

Further tax efficiencies are available as a result of the fact that legitimate business expenses such as equipment, travel costs and subsistence can be offset against the Corporation Tax paid by your limited company. This reduces the overall amount on which you have to pay tax. You can also reclaim VAT on certain business purchases.

The other great benefit is that the company profits can be reinvested in future entrepreneurial activity and do not have to all be taken as personal income.

**Get expert guidance to retain contractor status**

Managing your limited company according to the rules won't necessarily guarantee that you are taxed as an outside-IR35 limited company contractor. As we have mentioned, employment status is a matter of law. Each contract you undertake via your limited company needs to be approached with caution and you must carry out the necessary due diligence to ensure you remain outside IR35.

Fortunately, this is a relatively simple and inexpensive exercise, when you consider the tax savings you'll be making as a result. The first step when assessing a new contract is to have it evaluated online using an independent IR35 testing solution. ir35testing.co.uk is free-to-use and provides the most comprehensive and accurate evaluation available. Further expert guidance on carrying out your due diligence is provided in chapter 8.

## 2.4 Sole traders

The sole trader route isn't a particularly popular trading vehicle for contractors anymore, as it doesn't offer as many of the advantages of limited company contracting. Also, most clients will only engage with you if you operate via a limited company to avoid any associated tax risk when engaging sole traders. However, it's still very important for all parties involved to be able to distinguish a self-employed sole trader from a contractor, for a multitude of reasons.

For example, when engaging with a client, don't be surprised if they are blissfully unaware that there are different types of self-employment. Many employees will never have experienced anything other than employment themselves, in which case you will need to explain:

a) That you are not a sole trader
b) The differences between your working arrangement and that of a sole trader, notably the different tax treatment

It's also important to note that, if you sub-contract work to a sole trader and they don't pay the correct amount of income tax and NICs, you may find your limited company liable for the outstanding amount under the debt transfer legislation. This is one of the main reasons agencies and clients are often reluctant to engage with sole traders, as well as being a key motivator for contractors to incorporate.

## Sole traders are their own boss

Like limited company contractors, sole traders are their own boss and take responsibility for the success or failure of their business. They are responsible for paying their own income tax and NICs and are not subject to PAYE. Sole traders don't receive the employment rights available to employees.

Whilst employees are generally obliged to turn up for work every day, and expected to carry out the tasks assigned to them, sole traders have no such obligations. They are usually engaged to complete a specific service or project for a client and are only required to perform tasks related to the specific service or project that is described in their contract.

So, whereas an employment contract is a *contract of service* by an individual, the self-employed are usually hired to deliver a service and have a *contract for services*. This is a key distinction and you will see it referred to many times. A contract for services means that you could send someone else in to do the job, meaning the ability to substitute is present. Substitution is a hugely important factor in IR35 and employment case law.

## Indicators of self-employment

The important indicators for the worker of being self-employed include:

- Personal service/substitution: No personal requirement - can send substitute
- Control: not controlled by the client
- Mutuality of obligation: not obligation for any work to be offered or accepted
- Financial risk: own money risked and opportunity to gain financially
- Being in business on your own account: seen to be running a legitimate business
- Part and parcel: isn't a 'fixture' of the client's organisation
- Provision of equipment: can use own equipment to carry out the job

Of these factors, although all can play a part, the first three are the most critical in determining whether or not your contract is caught by IR35. For a more comprehensive overview of the factors determining your status, visit chapter 5.

Sole traders are not taxed at source like employees. They add up income earned during the tax year and deduct expenses, and then pay income tax and NICs on their profits. This is all done via the self-assessment tax system which applies to sole traders and anyone else who earns money and does not have it deducted at source.

## 2.5 Workers

Beyond employment and self-employment, there is a third statutory definition of employment, the 'worker'. As a limited company contractor you may be wondering what relevance worker status has on your bearing as being outside IR35. The truth is it can play an influential part in the negotiation process at the beginning of a new contract.

Contractors have occasionally been known to use the threat of employment rights to force through amends to their contracts with agencies and clients. This happens where a contract initially more closely resembles that of a worker who is eligible for certain employment rights, and not a contractor.

If you find that an agency or client is playing hardball during negotiations, suggesting that you may claim worker status and the associated employment rights could be all you need to secure an outside-IR35 contract. Firstly, you need to understand the definition in itself.

**What is a 'worker'?**

Workers engage in temporary work, but their working practices may more closely reflect those of an employee. Worker is a statutory definition, and the distinction between contractor and worker was summarised in the Supreme Court case of Bates van Winkelhof-v-Clyde & Co LLP and another [2014] by Baroness Hale:

*"One kind are people who carry on a profession or a business undertaking on their own account and enter into contracts with clients or customers to provide work or services for them [contractors]. The other kind are self-employed people who provide their services as part of a profession or business undertaking carried on by someone else [workers]."*

There are certain indicators that define a worker. These include:

- A contract to perform work or services personally for a reward which is either money or a benefit in kind
- A limited right to send someone else to carry out the work
- Mutuality of obligation
- Not doing the work as part of their own limited company in an arrangement where the 'employer' is actually a customer or client

These may conflict with the description of a contractor, but what is written into a contract isn't final. When HMRC, and potentially later a tax tribunal, consider IR35 status, they look at the 'notional contract'. This is an evaluation of the real-life working practices gauged from the written contracts as well as other evidence. If the notional contract indicates that a contractor's working arrangements do not align with the written contract, the written contract will be overruled.

Workers are entitled to certain employment rights available to employees, such as:

- National minimum wage
- Protection against unlawful deductions from wages
- Protection against unlawful discrimination
- Statutory minimum level of paid holiday

**Don't try and self-classify your status**

One example of a contract of self-employment being overturned to grant individuals worker status comes from the employment tribunal Aslam, Farrar and Others v Uber [2016]. Here, two Uber drivers were deemed eligible to claim employment rights after the written contract was considered not to reflect the reality of the working relationship.

However, the important thing to note is a huge amount of paperwork and evidence had to be examined for the judge to reach their verdict. This is because of the substantial amount of case law that underpins employment status. You should never attempt to self-classify your status. When determining whether IR35 applies, due diligence is always required.

Your first port of call should be to get an online IR35 evaluation from an independent source. The best IR35 test on the internet is ir35testing.co.uk. Following this, you should have an IR35 expert perform a contract review for you. This way you can gain certainty over your IR35 status, as well as evidence to mount a strong defence should HMRC ever challenge you. Further guidance on conducting due diligence is provided in chapter 8.

## 2.6 The differences between each working model summarised

It's important to understand the key differences between each working model in order to help ensure that neither your contract nor your real-life working arrangements deviate from what is expected of a limited company contractor. Table 2.1 details the fundamental differences between each working model.

| | Permanent employee | Self-employed (sole trader) | Worker | Limited company |
|---|---|---|---|---|
| Contract type | Contract of service | Contract for services | Contract of service | Contract for services |
| Permanent or temporary? | Permanent | Temporary | Temporary | Temporary |
| Does the worker have employment rights? | Yes | No | Some limited rights | No |
| Means of taxation | PAYE | Via self-assessment | Via self-assessment or PAYE | Via self-assessment |
| Is the worker controlled? | Yes | No | Yes | No |
| Does the worker have a right of substitution? | No | Yes | Limited | Yes |
| Does MOO exist? | Yes | Sometimes | Yes | Sometimes |
| Affected by IR35? | No | No | No | Yes |

Table 2.1 The key differences between each working model.

## 2.7 Chapter summary – key lessons for contractors, agencies and clients

### Contractors

- Employment status is not a choice, but a matter of law, and is defined by both the contractual agreement and the ongoing working practices.

- Though definitions of employment types exist, the interpretations of policymakers, HMRC, tax law experts and employment law experts often differ, causing confusion.

- Limited company contracting is the most tax-efficient and lucrative trading option for contractors. But it is the working arrangements that can be targeted for IR35.

### Agencies

- There are numerous subtle differences between each type of contract, and what is written down doesn't necessarily define the working arrangements.

- Substitution, control and mutuality of obligations (MOO) are the three most important factors determining whether or not the worker is caught by IR35.

- There are several amendments a contractor will want to negotiate into a contract to indicate that the working arrangement doesn't resemble employment, which you shouldn't be afraid to agree to.

## Clients

- Exerting too much control over how a contractor carries out their work when contracting with you directly puts them at risk of IR35.

- Limited company contractors will want to engage with you on a contract for services via their company, meaning they aren't obliged to provide the services personally.

- The contract between your organisation and contractor should avoid including any form of employment rights whatsoever, or else IR35 will apply.

# 3

# What clients and agencies need to know about IR35

# 3.1 IR35 – why does it matter to clients and agencies?

Having read chapters 1 and 2, you will understand IR35 and that, from April 2017, it is no longer solely a problem for contractors. Historically they have been responsible for ensuring they comply with the legislation and liable for any backdated tax, penalties and interest if they are found to be non-compliant. This is no longer the case from April 2017.

**Public sector changes – who does what?**

New rules from April 2017 make contractor clients in the public sector responsible for IR35 compliance. Where an agency is involved in the supply chain, they are responsible for calculating, reporting and paying tax on each payment made to the contractor. This includes paying employer's National Insurance (NI) themselves, if the client concludes that the contractor is caught by IR35.

If the contractor contracts direct with the client, the client will take on this responsibility instead. HMRC is yet to confirm who will be responsible for backdated tax, penalties and interest when an incorrect IR35 judgement is made. However, it is likely either the client or the agency (if there is one) will be picking up the bill.

This means agencies are faced with substantial costs processing contractors inside IR35, and either the client or the agency could also risk mammoth tax penalties in the instance that HMRC challenges an IR35 decision. So, public sector recruitment agency or client, IR35 has become your problem too.

**Private sector – no change, yet**

For clients and agencies in the private sector, from April 2017 the rules will stay the same as they have always been, for the time being. Private sector contractors will retain responsibility for IR35 compliance and will be liable for any outstanding tax, penalties and interest if it is found that they have been non-compliant.

Whilst HMRC has stated that the new rules are strictly intended for the public sector, IR35 experts are unanimous in their belief that a private sector roll out isn't far behind. This means all contractor clients and agencies may have to get to grips with the new rules.

Either way, this chapter will still prove useful in helping you to understand more about IR35, why a contractor may wish to negotiate changes to their contract, and what processes are necessary to help guarantee compliance.

## 3.2 Why agencies and/or clients are responsible for IR35 compliance from April 2017 [Public sector bodies only]

Most contractors who trade via limited companies do so to engage with clients who want an arms-length business-to-business relationship. In most instances, this is the preferred set-up for contractor, client and agency. However, judging from the taxman's enthusiasm for enforcing IR35, HMRC believes tax avoidance is the key motivator for contractors.

This is largely down to the taxman's perception that there is significant tax lost due to IR35 not being operated properly by many limited company contractors. With self-employment increasingly popular, National Insurance Contributions (NICs), and in particular Employers NI, are diminishing, heightening the taxman's concerns. Contrary to both what case law says and to the Government's often quoted intentions to encourage small businesses through the tax system, HMRC believes that two workers doing the same job should be taxed the same.

This sounds logical, until you realise that limited company contractors do not receive any of the employment benefits available to employees such as holiday pay, sick pay and access to an employee pension scheme, amongst others. Neither do contractors experience the job security that employees enjoy. On top of that the Government has historically always supported entrepreneurship, which includes small businesses and contractors, through the tax system.

**How big does HMRC think the problem is?**

HMRC perceives IR35 to be a far bigger problem than many experts believe.

HMRC's consultation on the public sector reforms[1] in 2016 estimated that non-compliance was set to cost the Exchequer £440m in the 2016/17 tax year. This was in spite of a Public Accounts Committee (PAC) report[2] published on 13 April 2016 which found that in fact 90% of public sector contractors had their tax affairs in order.

Nonetheless, HMRC maintains that stricter enforcement of IR35 is necessary. So, in the March 2016 Budget the Chancellor announced that reforms of IR35 in the public sector would be legislated and enacted in April 2017.

Despite criticism from contracting stakeholders and tax and accountancy bodies such as the Association of Chartered Certified Accountants (ACCA) and the Association of Accounting Technicians (AAT), the Chancellor announced in the November 2016 Autumn Statement that the plans were going ahead.

Draft legislation swiftly followed and was released on 5 December 2016, providing further details of the changes and their substantial impact on the public sector supply chain.

## A bigger impact – the private sector?

The reforms mean that what has only been a concern for contractors in the past now impacts further down the public sector supply chain, affecting contractor recruitment agencies and end clients. With experts warning that expansion of the new rules into the private sector will follow, all agencies and contractor clients will have to comply with the complicated legislation that has troubled contractors for so long.

The logic behind this warning largely stems from the anticipated tax yield from the public sector measures. In the 2016 Autumn Statement it was confirmed that the taxman expects to bring in £25m in additional tax receipts in the 2017/18 tax year, falling to £20m in 2018/19.

With this making up such a small portion of the supposed £440m that the taxman loses to IR35 non-compliance, are we really expected to believe that HMRC won't go after the majority with a private sector roll out?

1. HMRC, *Off-payroll working in the public sector: reform of the intermediaries legislation*
2. House of Commons Committee of Public Accounts, *Use of consultants and temporary staff*

## 3.3 New rules bring in compliance requirements for public sector engagers [Public sector bodies only]

Prior to April 2017, the rules in both the private and public sectors mean contractors are responsible for their IR35 compliance, conducting due diligence by correctly checking their IR35 status, and paying the relevant tax and NICs when they fall within its scope.

However, from April 2017 the client is responsible for checking IR35 status and enforcing the legislation where necessary. Where a contractor is judged to be caught by IR35, in most cases it is up to the public sector agency to calculate, report and pay tax and NICs to HMRC via real time information (RTI). This includes paying employer's NI. If there is no agency involved in the supply chain, the public sector client takes on this responsibility.

HMRC is yet to confirm who will be liable for tax, penalties and interest should the taxman challenge an outside-IR35 status decision, but many expect that it will either be the client or agency. Clients will also need to make sure that they have compliance and testing procedures in place to reassess contractors at times of renewal. If a contractor enters a contract as outside IR35, they don't expect their status to change midway through. As such, the client needs to be diligent in ensuring this doesn't happen.

**Decision time for public sector clients**

Public sector clients now have a big decision to make. Many will be tempted to avoid the administrative burden and tax risk by only offering inside-IR35 contracts. However, this will likely result in a sharp fall in contractor engagement. Most contractors won't work for up to 20% less, which is what being found inside IR35 could mean.

Being able to provide an honest assessment of a contractor's IR35 status within a public sector context could become a major competitive advantage. Clients and agencies that are willing to invest time and effort into implementing a smooth IR35 assurance process will attract more contractors. For most public sector clients, using an outsourced solution, such as ir35testing.co.uk, will be the most efficient and cost-effective option.

It's also important to remember that the consensus amongst experts is that HMRC intends to roll out the legislation into the private sector. So, private sector firms and agencies who engage contractors could also be subject to these changes.

**The cost of non-compliance**

The cost of falling within IR35 is significant, and can result in up to a 20% reduction in net pay, depending on the contractor's income. However, the cost of non-compliance or an incorrect judgement is even greater, potentially running to tens of thousands of pounds. The taxman may issue a demand for back taxes and NICs and can add penalties of up to 70% of the unpaid tax.

Whilst the burden on contractors is huge, from April 2017 the same may be said for public sector clients and agencies who could potentially find themselves liable for five figure sums per contractor, per year, if they get the IR35 status wrong.

Who is liable for unpaid tax, penalties and interest as the result of an incorrect IR35 judgement has not yet been confirmed by HMRC. However, it is expected that it will be either the client or the agency. Public sector bodies need to mitigate their risk, which makes it essential to undertake strict compliance procedures to ensure every IR35 judgement is the correct one.

# 3.4 Public sector clients – a warning about the Employment Status Service

To ease the burden on public sector clients, HMRC is releasing its own Employment Status Service (ESS) tool to help determine a contractors IR35 status. The tool takes the form of an online questionnaire and the taxman has already stated that it intends to be bound by the judgement delivered by it on each contractor's status. That means using the ESS should ensure your firm avoids any dispute with the taxman over status, and so at face value it may appear to be a simple, risk-free solution.

The problem is that the ESS tool is skewed towards delivering a 'fail' outcome, even when a contractor is likely to have passed IR35. This is because the tool is based on the taxman's interpretation of how IR35 should be applied, rather than the case law that underpins the legislation, as experts who have seen the ESS have pointed out. HMRC has said many times, contrary to actual case law, that people doing the same kind of work should pay the same level of tax – but that's not actually the law.

## IR35 is subjective

IR35 is highly subjective. Whilst there are certain factors that alone may indicate that a contractor is either inside or outside IR35, other factors may make it more or less likely that they are caught. As such, IR35 status, or risk, needs to be displayed along a spectrum. The ESS doesn't do this, yet the taxman claims it will still be able to provide upfront certainty as to a contractor's IR35 status.

If a contractor receives a low risk result on a spectrum, it stands to reason that they have a very good chance of passing IR35. The ESS, on the other hand, will simply present one of two results – pass or fail - and to provide a pass result it would require absolute certainty. But absolute certainty is an extreme rarity in a subjective test such as IR35. The only way the ESS can provide absolute certainty is by failing every contractor that it itself isn't 100% certain about. As such, contractors shouldn't expect to receive a pass from HMRC very often. Ultimately, for a result that is not legally binding, the ESS will prove more trouble than it's worth for users.

## Contractors to steer clear of the Employment Status Service

The contract sector is well aware of the inadequacies of the ESS, and many contractors are likely to refuse to use it. A July 2016 survey conducted by this book's publisher ContractorCalculator found that 80% of contractors said they would seek out private sector opportunities if deemed to be inside IR35, which is the major concern for the public sector.

The ESS won't cause any financial risk to your organisation, but it may deter contractors from engaging with your firm. The only way to minimise your risk and continue to engage the contractors you need is to conduct your own due diligence and follow the steps laid out in this chapter.

## 3.5 Ensuring IR35 compliance – necessary steps [Public sector bodies only]

### Evaluate IR35 status using ir35testing.co.uk

You have a far better chance of reaching an accurate IR35 status decision if you obtain an independent evaluation. This way, your contractor is happy you've taken the necessary measures to reach a sound judgement and your own risk is minimalised, as you will have taken the advice of an IR35 specialist. This can all be at no extra cost to your organisation, which can offset any costs onto the contractor.

The first step is to have the contractor evaluate their status online using an independent IR35 testing solution. This is a fast and efficient method of mass testing contractors, ensuring any administrative workload is kept to a minimum.

The most comprehensive IR35 test on the market is ir35testing.co.uk. Built by ContractorCalculator in 2009, the underlying test has been accessed by over 100,000 contractors. Based on comprehensive knowledge of IR35 since its inception in April 2000 and decades of employment case law expertise, ir35testing.co.uk is clinically accurate, with the test algorithm frequently updated to align with the latest IR35 tax tribunal outcomes.

Unlike the ESS, which will simply deliver a pass or fail verdict, ir35testing.co.uk displays the contractor's IR35 risk on a spectrum, allowing you to make an informed decision regarding the contractor's status and your next steps. As well as a case-law backed assessment, compliance advice is also available for the contractor. Evidence of taking the test is also useful as a means of demonstrating due diligence.

**Have the contractor get a professional contract review**

If the contractor stands a decent chance of passing IR35, you should encourage them to seek a professional contract review from an IR35 specialist. This demonstrates both due diligence and reasonable care in HMRC's eyes and will provide you with factual evidence that will help mount a strong defence if HMRC challenges you, not that they should if you have followed the advice of the expert.

When having a contract reviewed by a specialist, make sure:

- They are an IR35 specialist with the necessary employment legislation expertise and not a high street solicitor
- They have a proven track record in evaluating IR35 contract risks and specific experience in the contract sector.

The IR35 specialist may suggest amendments to the contract to make it more IR35-friendly, further minimising the risk of the contractor being caught. You shouldn't be afraid to agree to these, as no changes suggested by the specialist will be to the detriment of your organisation.

Following these steps will ensure you have taken the necessary steps to appease your contractor without placing your organisation at risk of tax and penalties. These steps are explained in more detail in section 8.3.

**Don't be afraid of a confirmation of arrangements**

Another measure necessary to ensuring your contractor can achieve an IR35-compliant contract without putting your organisation at risk is agreeing and signing a confirmation of arrangements. Amongst other details, a confirmation of arrangements will typically highlight:

- The precise nature of the services provided
- That a substitute chosen by the contractor can be supplied, at their expense
- That you do not have excessive control over how, when and where the contractor completes their work
- That the contractor doesn't take on work not specified in the contract.

Don't worry. This isn't an attempt by the contractor to flaunt their responsibilities. Rather it is a written statement confirming elements of the arrangements proving that the contractor is outside IR35 that aren't stipulated in the contract. If HMRC ever challenge a contractor's status, this document will prove a vital part of your body of evidence in a successful defence. Again, you'll want to ensure that the contractor obtains expert help in putting together the confirmation of arrangements to ensure it matches the real-life working practices, therefore further minimising your risk.

Alternatively, if you choose to test a contractor's IR35 status online with ir35testing.co.uk, your contractor can purchase a status report which includes a sign off sheet that you can sign to confirm their working arrangements, as indicated by the outcome of the test. This can prove very useful and will bulk up your body of evidence ready for the taxman.

**Make sure everyone sticks to the contract**

With the shift in compliance burden and likely transfer of tax liability, you'll need to be extra vigilant in ensuring that the working relationship doesn't deviate from what is written down on paper, or risk facing huge sums in tax, penalties and interest.

Remember, a contract can be agreed with all the necessary clauses and inclusions to indicate that a contract for services has been agreed between two businesses, but it is meaningless if the parties involved don't abide by it. When negotiating a contract, a contractor will typically wish to demonstrate that:

- There is a right of substitution
- The client has no control over the manner in which the contractor carries out the work
- There is no mutuality of obligation between the contractor and client

However, in an IR35 investigation, HMRC looks at the notional contract, which is the contract in force based on the real relationship between the contractor and client, established by gathering key evidence from the contractor, client, agency and other relevant parties. The notional contract is also what is considered by tax tribunal judges, so this step is critical.

# 3.6 How IR35 experts determine IR35 status

There are three key elements to IR35 which play a large part in deciding whether a contractor's contract is caught by the legislation. These are:

- **Substitution** – regarded as IR35's silver bullet, if a contractor has the right to send a substitute in their place, this suggests that personal service does not apply and the worker cannot possibly be an employee

- **Control** – if the client exerts a significant amount of control over what work the contractor carries out, and when, where and how it is done, it's an indication that the contractor could be inside IR35

- **Mutuality of obligation (MOO)** – MOO by itself will not determine the nature of a contract as it can be present in both a contract of service and a contract for services. If the contractor passes the above two tests, MOO is unlikely to factor as the contractor will likely be deemed outside IR35. However, it remains one of the key tests of employment status.

There are other indicators that the relationship between the worker and the end-user client is one of employment, and therefore inside IR35. These factors carry far less weight than the three key elements, although they also need to be considered. They include:

- Financial risk
- Being in business on one's own account
- Provision of equipment by the contractor,
- The contractor becoming "Part and parcel" of the organisation

These are all explained in greater detail in chapter 5 of this book.

Ultimately though, IR35 is a complex legislation to enforce, and ensuring compliance requires extensive know-how. Public sector agencies and clients will likely find that they either need to hire an in-house expert who understands IR35, or outsource their compliance procedure to a third party solution.

Fortunately, expert help is available at affordable prices. The cloud based service ir35testing.co.uk is a compliance solution that is free for agencies and clients, and helps determine the IR35 status of contractors without creating an excessive administrative burden.

## 3.7 What happens if a contractor is inside IR35?

**Public sector**

After a determination by the public sector client that IR35 applies to a contract, the party who then has the responsibility for making the necessary tax deductions depends on the supply chain. HMRC states that, where the contractor contracts with the client via a recruitment agency, it is the agency's responsibility to deduct the necessary tax and NICs at source via Pay As You Earn (PAYE) on any payment made to the contractor's limited company. Should the contractor contract directly with the client, from April 2017 it will be the client's responsibility to tax the contractor. To do this, the agency or client is required to gather certain personal details from the contractor, including:

- Their name
- Their address
- Their National Insurance number

HMRC instructs that the agency or client calculates, reports and pays the relevant tax via Real Time Information (RTI). This is likely to cause problems because many agencies and clients will be required to join up separate systems for payroll and for paying invoices. As is the case now, the contractor's limited company will continue to be responsible for VAT. With this responsibility also comes the burden of paying employer's NI on payments made to the contractor. Experts warn that this will significantly impact agency margins, which are likely to be renegotiated as a result, most likely at the expense of the client.

HMRC also appears to have overlooked the fact that public sector agencies and clients will rarely be able to make the correct calculation on behalf of the contractor. Experts have pointed out that agencies and clients will be required to account for all allowable deductions, including pension contributions, expenses and capital allowances, when calculating a contractor's tax liability. However, this information won't be readily available when needed. The fallout from this is that the contractor accountants will assume a heavier workload as they seek to correct each calculation. Therefore, it is in every party's best interests to ensure that the contractor can compliantly achieve an outside-IR35 contract.

Being able to provide an outside-IR35 contract is all-the-more important as it is extremely unlikely that a contractor would agree to an alternative arrangement. There are numerous reasons why. When offered an inside-IR35 contract, a public sector contractor might reply:

- "The process is too complex, and it would be cheaper for me to provide my services through an umbrella company."
- "If you want to hire me as an employee, then place me on a fixed term employment contract with employee rights."
- "If you wish to tax me as an employee without employment rights I'm afraid I'm going to have to increase my rates."
- "I'm going to have to decline the contract. I'm going to try my luck in the private sector."

As a result, being able to prove that a contractor is outside IR35 has arguably never been more important for public sector agencies and clients.

## Private sector

If you are a contractor agency or client in the private sector, IR35 compliance is the responsibility of the contractor. No input is required from you on determining status or calculating, reporting and paying tax. However, if a contractor considers their contract to be caught by IR35, there is a good chance that they will approach the agency or client in the hope that changes can be made.

If they have conducted their necessary due diligence, the contractor will have secured a contract review from an IR35 specialist. The expert will either have instructed them on what amendments need to be made to the contract to get them outside IR35, or will approach the agency or client directly with proposed changes.

These changes will often be small and won't significantly impact the working arrangements themselves. Typically, a contractor will seek to amend wording in the contract to indicate certain factors that imply that they are outside IR35. For example, amongst other details they may request that the contract specifies:

- The precise nature of the services provided
- The fact that they work according to their own hours
- The fact they have an unfettered right to substitute
- The fact that they are not under any significant control
- Confirmation that they aren't governed by the same rules as permanent employees.

If you're the recruitment agent, the likelihood is you'll have other things to worry about, and you may believe there is no benefit to your organisation in renegotiating a contract. However, negotiating IR35 compliance with a contractor could be the difference between you securing the placement and the contractor testing the waters elsewhere.

If market conditions mean significant demand for their services, this risk is intensified.

If you're a private sector contractor client, there is a chance that the contractor will approach you directly if the agency refuses to budge on the contract. In which case, you might be well advised to speak to the agency and encourage them to come to an agreement with the contractor.

This will be even more important if the contractor has a unique skillset making them difficult to replace. Beware, failure to negotiate with the contractor could see them walk out the door.

# 3.7 Chapter summary – key lessons for contractors, agencies and clients

## Contractors

- The introduction of the public sector reform results from HMRC's difficulties with enforcing the legislation itself and its mistaken view that IR35 non-compliance is far more prevalent than it is.

- If caught by IR35, you can suffer a reduction in net pay of up to 20%.

- If you are a public sector contractor, your client is required to assess your IR35 status. It's important to work with the client and conduct your due diligence to secure an outside-IR35 contract and prove it to HMRC should you be challenged.

## Agencies

- Reform to IR35 in the public sector means agencies need to calculate, report and deduct tax for each public sector contractor they engage who is caught by IR35.

- HMRC instructs that tax is reported and paid via RTI. This brings with it a sizeable administrative burden that you may need to outsource.

- IR35 is determined by the ongoing working practices between the contractor and client, so the agency-contractor contract alone can't guarantee IR35 compliance.

## Clients

- From April 2017, contractor clients in the public sector are responsible for checking the IR35 status of contractors.

- Public sector clients who are willing to invest time and effort into implementing a smooth IR35 assurance process will gain a source of competitive advantage and will attract more contractors.

- There are various ways to mitigate the risk of IR35, including using free, independent IR35 testing tools and professional contract reviews.

# 4

# Current HMRC guidance on IR35

4. Current HMRC guidance on IR35

# 4.1 Using HMRC guidance on IR35

HMRC has a wealth of online information, guidance and resources concerning IR35. Its resources include the practitioners' manuals that HMRC inspectors use to help determine a contractor's IR35 status, which include examples of various scenarios and explanations detailing how HMRC will evaluate whether or not IR35 applies.

HMRC's material is generally useful as it provides contractors with insights into how the taxman might apply IR35 in their personal circumstances. For contractors new to IR35, HMRC's online guidance, 'IR35 (intermediaries legislation): find out if it applies', explains when IR35 needs to be considered and the penalties for not following IR35 rules. It also advises on next steps for contractors looking to find out whether the legislation applies.

**Treat HMRC guidance with caution**

However, you should be wary about applying HMRC's guidance, as it does not always align with the actual legislation. There are grey areas where HMRC's view is that IR35 would apply without question, whereas an independent IR35 specialist and a tax tribunal may disagree with the taxman's interpretation of the law. So, whilst mostly accurate, you should treat it with some caution, as HMRC is not always right, despite what an inspector would have you believe.

You should be even more cautious when using HMRC's IR35 helpline and contract review service. Or better yet, don't use them at all. Though the taxman claims that information shared via the IR35 helpline and contract review service is confidential and isn't shared with its compliance teams, there are plenty of better alternatives for information on IR35 and contract reviews. And some experts claim to have evidence of unusual correlations between their contractor clients having used HMRC's services then being the subject of an investigation that appears remarkably perceptive.

Similarly, you shouldn't use HMRC's guidance as a substitute for adopting IR35 best practice, or as an excuse not to invest in a contract review or investigation insurance. Both are readily affordable and a small portion of the sum you will save in tax by legitimately proving that your contract is outside IR35.

You have been warned.

# 4.2 HMRC's Employment Status Manual

Though HMRC's Employment Status Manual provides resources to determine the employment status of all kinds of workers – be they employed, workers, self-employed sole traders, etc. - it is these same broad and complex employment status tests that determine whether a contractor is caught by IR35. The fact that they rely on the same legislation and case law makes the Employment Status Manual, which is also the guidance used by HMRC's own compliance officers, an extremely useful point of reference for contractors.

The guidance used by HMRC compliance teams to enforce IR35 is found in section ESM3000. This provides a comprehensive overview of the legislation, highlighting the basic principles of IR35, including when it applies, employment status legislation case law and its relevance, deemed payment, and application of tax and NICs rules.

**Comparing the evidence**

Particularly important is the section titled 'comparing the evidence'. This explains how HMRC inspectors can apply the relevant tax legislation and tests of employment – such as control, mutuality of obligation and substitution – to determine a contractor's IR35 status. Being able to observe and assess the aspects of a contract considered to be important by an HMRC inspector by way of reading this section should help you to come to a sound judgement regarding your status.

UK law is based on common law and precedent, therefore past legal cases play a significant part in determining the verdict in each individual IR35 case. The same is true of tax and employment law. It is for this reason that HMRC also includes an extensive reference section of relevant case law summaries (found in ESM7000).

This section is updated every time new decisions concerning case law are reached in court or tax tribunals, with updates including commentary on how decisions are expected to impact on future and ongoing cases. It provides a critical resource for contractors seeking to understand how the legislative framework is changing and how the courts would come to a judgement.

# 4.3 IR35 case study examples

Interestingly, the Employment Status Manual also includes a section titled 'opinions on contracts', which includes three example case studies to help guide decisions made in practice by compliance officers, highlighting what factors determine the contractor's status in each scenario. The range of determining factors mentioned in each case study, which we have provided an overview of below, go to show the complexity of the legislation and provide an important point of reference for contractors.

**Case study 1: Gordon – inside IR35**

For example, Gordon is an IT contractor who works through his own limited company. Gordon is working on a six month contract as part of a support team for the client's payroll system. Gordon's team leader tells him what work he is to carry out at any particular time, whilst the client has the right to tell Gordon 'how' the work should be carried out. Gordon is required to work forty hours each week at the client's premises.

Gordon's company is contracted to supply Gordon to carry out the work personally using equipment and materials supplied by the client and neither has the right to terminate the contract early. These are but a few of the full range of factors considered in the case study example.

HMRC concludes that, in this instance, Gordon is caught by IR35 as the engagement would have been one of employment had it been direct between Gordon and the client, adding: 'The only pointers to self-employment are the minimal financial risk (from invoicing), the ability to work for others (again, a minor point) and the existence of a business organisation/work for other clients.'

**Case study 2: Henry – outside IR35**

In another case study, Henry is a consultant engineer working through his own limited company who has been commissioned by a manufacturing company to produce a report on how its production line can increase productivity on a three month contract. Henry has a free hand over how his work is carried out and when, provided it meets the three month deadline. However, Henry is required to keep the client fully informed about progress and the client can require Henry to modify proposals if needed.

The only significant equipment Henry uses is his own computer to prepare the report, whilst he carries out 70% of the work in his office. There is no restriction imposed by the contract that prevents Henry's company from providing services to others during the engagement, and the engagement itself cannot be terminated early other than following a breach of contract.

HMRC concludes that IR35 does not apply in this example, with the main determining factor being the limited amount of control that the client can exert. Henry's provision of own equipment and the use of his own office for the majority of the work also points towards self-employment.

**Case study 3: Charlotte - borderline**

The final example describes the working arrangement of Charlotte, an IT consultant providing services through her own limited company to a software company. Charlotte has been engaged for her programming skills to work on a specific project as part of a team developing a new piece of software.

Charlotte writes sub-programs allocated by the client's project manager who specifies the way in which each sub-program is structured and can require changes to be made to the work carried out. The project is expected to last for three months and Charlotte works a set number of hours each week on a flexible basis.

Charlotte invoices for £3,600 every four weeks and makes her own provisions for holiday and sick pay through her own company. She also carries out some work for another client during weekends.

HMRC's view is that in this instance Charlotte's case is borderline. It points towards an 'extensive right of control' over Charlotte, highlighting the client's right to specify how work can be done and the fact that Charlotte is contracted to do the work personally with equipment supplied by the client.

However, it also points towards the variety of different engagements that Charlotte holds as an indicator of self-employment, as well as the risk from invoicing. And whilst HMRC notes that control is extensive, it is 'not total' as Charlotte cannot be directed to work on another project.

## 4.4 Be wary of HMRC's contract review service and helpline

HMRC launched a contract review service and IR35 helpline when IR35 was first introduced in 2000, but evidence obtained through a Freedom of Information Act (FOI) request by ContractorCalculator suggests that take-up then had been low.

One of the reasons is that HMRC seeks to contact end-clients to establish the exact nature of the working relationship, which is so important in determining IR35 status. Unsurprisingly, few contractors choose to have an HMRC inspector asking their clients detailed questions about the exact nature of their working relationships.

HMRC insists that its confidential IR35 helpline is independent and does not share information with its compliance teams. However, given that in May 2012 it launched a major compliance campaign supported by three dedicated teams based in Salford, Croydon and Edinburgh, each with a dozen inspectors and a status specialist, contractors have a right to be dubious. Furthermore, as highlighted above, experts believe that the helpline operation and HMRC's compliance teams are not entirely separated, as the taxman claims.

### Is it really in confidence?

If, during a helpline call, it becomes apparent that the contractor concerned is clearly inside IR35, is it realistic to expect the HMRC call handler – said by HMRC to be an IR35 compliance expert – to keep it to themselves? All organisations promote staff and move them around; so if a helpline IR35 expert is moved to an IR35 compliance team under pressure to scalp more IR35 heads, are they really going to avoid going after anyone they spoke to 'in confidence' on the helpline?

Should you use HMRC's contract review service and it concludes that your contract is outside IR35, you will receive a unique reference number. In practice, you would supply this reference when approached by HMRC and the review would be suspended whilst the taxman reviews your latest circumstances. This will remain valid for three years and could help close down any future enquiry, providing your circumstances don't change.

However, in the far more likely event that HMRC determines that you may be inside IR35, there is a very real risk that an enquiry will follow. The fact that HMRC only considers current contracts and not contracts that a contractor is considering adds further weight to the suggestion that the taxman is likely to act upon the outcomes determined by its contract review service.

**A worrying amount of information**

HMRC also requests a quite worrying amount of information from the contractor prior to reviewing the contract, adding:

"It's up to you to provide all the information. If you don't or can't do so, it may not be possible for HMRC to form an opinion."

The information requested includes, but is not limited to:

- Copies of the contracts
- Any documents relating to working terms and conditions
- Any written statements by the client or contractor about working practices
- Details of how the contractor found the contract, the recruitment process and a copy of the contract advert
- Any contractual details not actually written into the contract

- Other relevant information, such as the number of contracts completed during the year and the clients' details
- The contractor's National Insurance (NI) number, HMRC reference number and the contractor limited company's postcode.

If HMRC considers you are caught by IR35 and you dispute its judgement, the case will be passed onto one of the specialist compliance teams.

- This can only be done with your full permission.
- HMRC can contact your client to gain more information.
- You can appeal the verdict delivered by the IR35 inspector, but this would add significant time and expense.

As with the contract review service, don't even think about asking the helpline for a review. There are plenty of expert IR35 advisers out there who can do a better job for a reasonable fee and who prioritise only your interests. HMRC's conflict of interest means it won't provide you with advice on the steps you need to take to pass IR35. An independent expert will, and will help walk you through the process.

If you're concerned about a contract being caught by IR35, a good starting point is to visit the free online guides and resources available at ContractorCalculator, or test your contract for free at ir35testing.co.uk.

# 4.5 Chapter summary – key lessons for contractors, agencies and clients

## Contractors

- HMRC's Employment Status Manual contains the guidance used by HMRC's own compliance officers.

- Using HMRC's contract review service and IR35 helpline are not advised, as there are concerns about the confidentiality of information.

- The HMRC guidance is biased and doesn't always align with the actual law. Tax Tribunals have been known to disagree with the taxman's interpretation. Instead, use other independent resources like ContractorCalculator.co.uk

## Agencies

- HMRC's Employment Status Manual includes three example IR35 case studies. These are however very simplistic examples, and the underlying case law is extremely complex.

- The HMRC guidance is biased and doesn't always align with the actual IR35 legislation, so treat it with caution.

- To minimise risk, always use independent experts.

## Clients

- HMRC's Employment Status Manual provides some insight as to what an HMRC compliance officer might consider important when assessing a contractor's status.

- Do not encourage contractors to use HMRC's IR35 resources. It is biased and does not always align with the actual law. There are independent alternatives that can provide greater insight, like ContractorCalculator.co.uk.

- Adopt IR35 best practice by taking steps to help ensure that the contract falls outside IR35. Always use independent experts.

# 5

# Factors determining your IR35 status

# 5.1 Why you need to consider your IR35 status

IR35 has evolved since it first came into force in 2000. However, over the course of more than a decade-and-a-half, HMRC still hasn't found an effective way of enforcing it across the entire workforce.

The taxman's consultation on the public sector reforms[1] claims that there is 'widespread non-compliance', with only one in ten limited company contractors who should be operating the rules currently doing so, costing the Exchequer £440m in the 2016/17 tax year.

This is a bold claim, given that a Public Accounts Committee (PAC) report[2] published on 13 April 2016 found that 90% of public sector contractors provided satisfactory assurance that their tax affairs were in order. However, ineffective enforcement remains a key issue for IR35, which HMRC has chosen to address with the public sector reforms.

Whilst the changes have only been announced in the public sector, experts warn that a private sector rollout is likely to follow. In the 2016 Autumn Statement it was indicated that the measures would yield £25m in additional tax receipts in the 2017/18 tax year from some 20,000 non-compliant public sector contractors, and £20m in 2018/19. Given that this is only a small portion of HMRC's perceived tax shortfall as a result of non-compliance, expansion of the rules into the private sector looks extremely likely.

**Looking at the evidence**

The IR35 legislation is not just a simple list of do's and don'ts. When making a ruling in an IR35 case, a judge will consider all the evidence, including the contract itself and the contractor and client's working arrangements in practice.

So, to prepare an effective IR35 defence, you need as many 'contra-indicators' in place as possible. This is not about trying to prove that white is black or vice versa – if your contract means that you are effectively an employee then you must pay taxes as an employee. But if your contract places you outside IR35, you must ensure that there is no possible room for misinterpretation by a tax inspector or tax tribunal judge. That's what we'll go on to discuss.

## 5.2 IR35 – overview of key factors

Determining whether one of your contracts is caught by or 'inside' IR35 depends on whether there is evidence to suggest that you are a 'disguised employee'. This includes the terms and conditions in the contract, together with the contractor's actual working arrangements.

It is not the contractor being judged on IR35 status, but the specific contract. So, you could have three contracts in a year, two of which are outside IR35 and one inside.

When determining IR35 status, one has to stand back and consider the whole picture to arrive at the decision – that's what a tribunal judge will do if your case gets as far as a tax tribunal. But with this book you have all you need to prevent that from happening.

1. HMRC, *Off-payroll working in the public sector: reform of the intermediaries' legislation*
2. House of Commons Committee of Public Accounts, *Use of consultants and temporary staff*

The main factors in an IR35 decision are:

- Personal service / substitution – has the client hired your company or you personally?
- Control – does the client control you?

- Mutuality of obligation – are you obliged to accept work offered, and is the client obliged to offer you work?

These three factors – control, substitution or personal service, and mutuality of obligation –are often known as the 'tests of employment' and underpin all UK employment status cases, not just IR35 cases.

Other important factors include:

- Financial risk – do you risk your own money and is there opportunity for you to gain financially through sound management?
- Part and parcel – are you a 'fixture' of the client's organisation?
- Being in business on your own account – are you really running a business?
- Provision of equipment – do you use your own equipment to do the job?

If HMRC investigates and you are suspected of being a disguised employee and therefore incorrectly not paying enough tax, all these factors will be examined to decide your true IR35 status – firstly by an HMRC inspector and then, if you fight it, in a tax tribunal.

These factors are based on case law, which derives from previous employment status and tax cases that have been in the courts. These form the basis upon which your IR35 status rests, so are important to understand how we've got to where we are now.

## 5.3 IR35 case law and the tests of employment

There is no statutory definition in law for 'employment' and 'self-employment'. The definition of who is an employee and who is not depends heavily on case law, or jurisprudence, which is basically a set of principles of law established through precedent by judges over the years, decades and centuries.

HMRC itself makes this clear in its Employment Status Manual, which states:

*"'Office' and 'employment' are not defined in the legislation and the principles which determine whether an individual is an office holder or employee are derived from case law. In order to decide whether someone is employed or self-employed you have to obtain all of the relevant facts relating to the engagement and then interpret those facts in the light of this case law."*

It is this case law that is used to determine whether a contractor is either employed and inside IR35, or self-employed and outside IR35.

**Can you fight your corner?**

As a contractor, you don't need to learn all the employment status case law that underpins the rules for IR35. It is more productive for you to engage professional IR35 experts who specialise in employment law and IR35, although you should read on so that you understand the basics. Even if you decide to fight status disputes with HMRC yourself, your chance of success is low to virtually zero, which is why it's best left to the professionals. The costs of professional help can be insured against for only a small sum – circa £100.

However, even if the costs of your defence are covered by insurance, the time you spend on your defence, coupled with the stress and a potentially huge tax bill at the end, means the very best insurance is to not get yourself into bother in the first place. So, if you are investigated, make sure you have everything necessary ready to shut the investigation down quickly. When HMRC turn up and spring an attack, you should already have your armour to hand and be ready to fight.

The tests of employment applied to employment status cases and used by tax tribunal judges to determine a contractor's IR35 status arose from a famous employment status case known as the MacKenna's Ready Mixed Concrete ruling. Its full citation is "The judgment of MacKenna J. in Ready Mixed Concrete (South East) Ltd v Minister of Pensions and National Insurance [1968]".

In this ruling, Judge MacKenna laid down the key tests of employment a worker must pass in order that their status is that of an employee, and that an employment contract, or *contract of service* exists.

Judge MacKenna's specific words were:

*"A contract of service exists if these three conditions are fulfilled.*

> *(i)     The servant agrees that, in consideration of a wage or other remuneration, he will provide his own work and skill in the performance of some service for his master.*
>
> *(ii)    He agrees, expressly or impliedly, that in the performance of that service he will be subject to the other's control in a sufficient degree to make that other master.*
>
> *(iii)   The other provisions of the contract are consistent with its being a contract of service."*

All three of these conditions must be satisfied for a contract of service to exist.

From these conditions arise the key factors that determine IR35 status:

- Control
- Substitution
- Mutuality of obligation
- Other factors, such as financial risk, the opportunity to profit and so on.

These factors underpin your ability to demonstrate to an HMRC inspector or a tribunal judge that you are outside IR35. The difference is, to pass an IR35 test, a contractor must prove that the converse is true.

For example, they must demonstrate that the client isn't able to exert a significant amount of control over what work they complete, and how, when and where they complete it. In this chapter you will see each of these factors and how they impact your IR35 status.

Once you have seen the factors involved it is very useful for you to keep abreast of any IR35 or employment status cases that go through the courts to see if any precedents are set. There are only a handful of these each year and the results and analysis are widely reported. For coverage and expert analysis of the most recent cases visit ContractorCalculator.co.uk.

## 5.4 Notional contract – how working practices impact IR35 status

If a contract is badly written and contains elements indicating an employment type relationship, HMRC will flag this as a reason why the contractor must be inside IR35.

Unfortunately, ensuring a contract is well written and doesn't meet the key tests of employment won't necessarily guarantee a contractor protection from HMRC and IR35 either. Instead, HMRC will simply fall back on what is called the 'notional contract', or the hypothetical contract that is formed by the taxman after examining the true nature of the relationship between the contractor and the client.

Following a landmark employment status case in 2011, the 'Autoclenz ruling', an HMRC status inspector or tribunal judge now has the right to completely disregard the actual written contract. This is because, in a real world situation, the evidence to the contrary of the contract may be so compelling that the contract itself is deemed irrelevant. This reinforces the importance for contractors to maintain a paper trail documenting their working practices.

**Working out the real relationship**

This means HMRC inspectors and judges will look at what actually happens in the workplace and base much of their decision on testimony that reflects the day-to-day operations on the job. When judging a contractor's IR35 status, an inspector or judge will form a notional contract that expresses the real relationship between the contractor and client, which may contrast with what is written down.

So, a contractor may have a written contract with all the right clauses, but if the client thinks differently – and tells HMRC investigators that the actual working arrangements are different from the written contract – then the contractor could be in trouble.

There are also other important aspects that can't be written into a contract. The element of control, for example, is one of the most important factors when determining IR35 status. Control can't simply be defined by writing the extent to which it exists into a contract as it is determined by day-to-day working practices. Other smaller factors such as being 'part and parcel' of the organisation also cannot be determined by examining the contract.

More positively, the concept of the notional contract has saved many contractors from falling within IR35. A contractor whose contract did not explicitly include a substitution clause but actually used a substitute would be outside IR35. It's also been known for a contractor to conduct a substitution during an ongoing investigation, resulting in an immediate retreat and closure of the case by HMRC.

## Another defence – the written confirmation

The other defence against a badly worded contract is to seek a written "confirmation of arrangements" from the client. This provides additional information that would not usually be included in a contract, helping to clarify arrangements.

It can sometimes be challenging to convince a client to sign a confirmation of arrangements, and some may be reluctant to do so because of legal reasons. However, there are certain motivating factors which may encourage a client to sign in light of the public sector IR35 changes, including:

- Using the confirmation of arrangements to mitigate their tax risk
- Agreeing to a confirmation of arrangements to attract the engagement of more contractors

Further information on this topic is available in chapter 8.

## The upper level contract

HMRC will certainly want to see the agency-client contract, known as the 'upper level contract', while the contract between the contractor and the agency is known as the 'lower level contract'. This is another reason why the notional contract is so important.

If the upper level contract between the agency and the client differs from the lower level contract between the contractor and the agency – for example by not including a right of substitution – the notional contract could work to the contractor's advantage. This is why it is absolutely essential that your working practices don't deviate from what was agreed between you and the client or agency.

An added complication is that most contractors have no idea of the exact contractual relationship between their agency and client – the "upper contract". They also have little chance of securing a copy of what the agency and client rightly consider to be a confidential document.

## 5.5 'Contract for services' versus 'contract of service'

Understanding the types of contracts between, clients, agencies and contractors and employees is fundamental for a contractor to help determine and demonstrate whether they are inside or outside IR35.

### Contract for services

A *contract for services* is where the client or agency engages the contractor's limited company to provide services. The contractor then decides who is going to provide those services.

The contract should state the terms for the services that the company provides, but should try to avoid any mention of personal service. Though less prevalent nowadays, some clients will insist that the contractor is named in the contract, though it is important that any request to do so is resisted by the contractor. This is a strictly business-to-business engagement between two firms on a buyer and supplier basis which completely negates any question of an employment relationship.

The key aspects of a contractor's limited company engaged in a contract for services include:

- A requirement to supply services to the client according to the contract schedule's specification
- A requirement to provides services for the project specified in the contract
- A requirement to provide services to the standard required
- An obligation to correct any errors or defective work, without additional cost
- An agreed rate for the services in the contract
- The right to provide a substitute to complete the services specified in the contract
- Flexibility over how, when and where the services are provided

If either party fails to fulfil their obligations set out in the contract for services, they are in breach of contract and the other party can take legal action to remedy the situation.

This can be summarised by a contractor as: "Our firm is obliged to provide the services as set out in the schedule. Your firm cannot expect us to provide anything other than those services, nor choose who exactly should provide them."

**Contract of service**

A *contract of service* is where the client engages the worker as a named individual to provide services. This is the type of contract that employees have with their employer. If you have a contract of service with an organisation, you are very likely going to be caught by IR35.

Note that you might have a contract of service without realising it and without many of the benefits that employees have. Because IR35 looks at the working practices, your relationship with the client may include enough features of employment that HMRC, and potentially at a later date a tax tribunal, may deem you to be within IR35. This underlines the need to get professional advice on your status.

Below are the key rights and responsibilities afforded to an employee. The existence of any of these within your contract may indicate that you are engaged in a contract of service:

- The employee is controlled by the employer and must perform tasks as instructed by a line manager according to their job description
- The employee is required to work at a specific place during specific hours on specific days
- The employee cannot send anybody else in to work for them as a substitute
- Employees have statutory rights to holiday pay, sick pay, maternity and paternity rights and redundancy payments
- Employees have statutory rights regarding how they can be asked to leave their employment
- Employees aren't personally liable for any errors they make when completing work for their employer
- Employees may enjoy a range of additional benefits, such as company cars, private health insurance, health clubs, and so on.

In addition, a 'mutuality of obligation' (MOO) exists between the employee and employer. This means the employer is obliged to provide work for the employee, and the employee is obliged to undertake the work asked of them, or risk being dismissed. Similarly, if the employer does not fulfil their obligation to provide them with work, the employee can take action that might result in an industrial tribunal.

This is summarised more informally by an employee as: "I am obliged to turn up for work and you are obliged to find me work and pay me for it."

The presence of control, personal service and MOO is all that is required for IR35 to apply to a contract. However, being aware of the full extent of factors impacting each type of contract places you in a much better position to judge whether your employment status is affected by IR35.

## 5.6 Control

The issue of control is a key factor that determines whether or not you are an employee. HMRC's practitioner's guidance states that control may not necessarily be the determining factor in an IR35 case. However, recent tax tribunals and court cases involving IR35 have been dominated by the element of control, so its importance must not be underestimated.

The factor of control is typically broken down into four sub-factors:

- **What** work you are told to perform
- **When** you are told to perform the work
- **Where** you are told to perform the work, and
- **How** you should perform the work

You will often see the phase 'what, when, where and how' used by IR35 experts and in articles about IR35. If you think about your current or most recent contract in the context of these four sub-factors of control, you'll realise that you may have been under some degree of control by your client, but this does not necessarily mean you are caught by IR35.

Certain elements of control over the contractor can exist. For example, many contractors won't be able to help where or when they carry out their work, because they have to work on the client's site during certain working hours to be close to its infrastructure and staff. However, the last sub-factor is critical. Providing the client has no say over how the contractor completes their work once the schedule has been agreed, a contractor should safely pass this test.

Contractors tend to be highly knowledgeable specialists in a particular field. So, very few contractors are told *how* to perform their tasks, which is often a very critical control factor in IR35 cases. And if you are not controlled, the tests of employment are unlikely to indicate that you are an employee, meaning you are far more likely to pass IR35.

Clauses in the contract indicating that you must regularly report to the client might be construed as indicating control. The more that control is alluded to in the contract and the more control the client actually exercises, the more HMRC will believe you are an employee. Ideally you should be directed at the project to be worked on, given a brief, and then left to your own devices to complete the task.

Make it clear between yourself and the client from the offset that most decisions about how the service you deliver is provided are yours to make.

Where possible your contract should indicate that:

- You cannot be asked to do something not in your contract
- You're not governed by the same rules as permanent employees
- You can work from your home office
- You can work according to your own hours
- Projects in the contract are named, indicating that your company is providing services for a project of finite duration

The issue of control is a particularly large and complex area of employment law. It is one area in particular where you are advised to seek the input of a professional.

## 5.7 Substitution

The right of substitution has consistently been one of the central areas of focus for tribunal judges and a key factor that can place contractors outside IR35.

If you can provide a substitute, your personal service is clearly not required, so there cannot be an employment relationship, because that requires personal service. Making a genuine substitution is widely believed to be the single 'silver bullet' that will kill off any IR35 challenge by HMRC.

As a small business supplier to your client, if you are genuinely providing a service then another individual hired by your firm with your skill set able to provide the same service could take your place. A substitute qualifies as genuine when substituting for all or part of the work that the client is expecting to be completed.

However, there are further requirements necessary for a substitution to be considered genuine, as per employment case law. These are:

- The client must agree to the substitution
- The contractor must pay the substitute directly from their company
- It should be an 'unfettered' right, meaning the client cannot vet any replacement

But what if there is no substitute for you? If you are a famous television personality, a world-renowned expert on a recondite subject, or the last-surviving programmer in a software language that no one uses anymore, the interpretation of the court is likely to be that you have no possibility of substitution. However, this doesn't necessarily mean you are within IR35. The likelihood is that there is no element of control as your expertise means nobody else can instruct you on how to do your job.

On the other hand, if you have the right to replace yourself with another contractor who has much the same skills that you do, you are obviously not providing the services 'yourself', as an employee would. This strongly points away from employment and that you are outside IR35.

**You need to stay in control**

Remember, it's essential that you retain full control over any substitution. Clauses that require client approval or satisfaction are to be avoided. If the client has any control over the substitution process, the court will claim that the substitution is not an unfettered right and is therefore not valid. So, ensure you retain the right to find and furnish the substitute yourself in the contract – you must maintain an unfettered right of substitution.

An unfettered right of substitution can often be the critical factor in proving that a contractor is in business on their own account. The employment appeal tribunal UK Mail Ltd v Creasey [2012] is the perfect reinforcement of this.

The tribunal found that delivery driver Mr J Creasey was neither an employee of nor a worker for his client UK Mail Ltd and so couldn't claim unfair dismissal. This was determined because of the inclusion of the unfettered right of substitution in his contract. UK Mail Ltd did not have to agree to the suggested substitute or impose any tests on them, providing they met the basic occupational requirements for the role.

Though Mr Creasey claimed he was not aware of the clause, the fact that several other drivers had exercised their right of substitution was enough to suggest that the terms were not a sham, and so Mr Creasey was deemed to be self-employed.

**Reducing the risk of sending in a substitute**

If the client is not satisfied with the substitute's services, then your company is responsible no matter what and could be in breach of contract. You should at no time suggest that the client has control over the provision of services that you make.

Therefore, a relevant phrase in your contract might say something like: '...any costs incurred in providing a substitute will be at the expense of the Company.' This would nullify the risk of sending in a substitute who cannot do the job.

You also have the option of hiring a sub-contractor or helper to work on a specific contract. The distinctions between substitutes and subcontractors/helpers are important in the eyes of a tax tribunal or court, because they demonstrate different aspects of how you might be outside IR35 and not a disguised employee.

A substitute is usually considered a short-term fix to cover for you during periods of holiday, illness or other unexpected absence. An individual with the right skill set replaces you directly on the project for a short period, and the client is informed that a substitute is to be supplied by the contractor's limited company.

Helpers or subcontractors generally refers to additional workers that you use to perform tasks to help cope with periods of intense activity, or to lend specialist skills to one particular aspect of the project.

Subcontractors who have been engaged on a basis that is intrinsic to the completion of the contract, or where you need additional specialist skills to complete the project, are the most likely to be viewed by HMRC as evidence that you are not a disguised employee. Case law dating back 20 years recognises the importance of being able to provide a substitute and hiring helpers.

Tax experts all agree that if you can substitute then just do it – to prove that you can. It's the vital piece of evidence that will successfully combat any HMRC investigation.

# 5.8 Mutuality of obligation (MOO)

Mutuality of obligation (MOO) is one of the key tests of employment status, though less importance is placed upon it in court cases compared to control and substitution.

HMRC's definition of MOO says that:

"There must be an irreducible minimum of mutual obligation for there to be a contract of service. That irreducible minimum is:

- that the engager [client] must be obliged to pay a wage or other remuneration, and
- that the worker [contractor] must be obliged to provide his or her own work or skill.

However, the irreducible minimum could be present in either a contract of service or a contract for services and therefore, by itself, it will not determine the nature of a contract."

Under normal conditions of employment there is a mutuality of obligation between worker and employer. The employer is obliged to provide paid work for the employee, and the employee is obliged to accept it. There is an expectation of regular employment by the employee until they are either made redundant or leave of their own accord.

This situation is typical of most employer-employee relationships, in which the employee is paid by their employer each week or month and can be asked to undertake tasks across a spectrum of activities that go beyond their core role.

Once the irreducible minimum of mutual obligation has been established, the key to distinguishing between a services contract and an employment contract, the

irreducible minimum requirements for a contract of
employment must be considered. These are:

- the requisite mutuality of obligation present;
- a sufficient degree of control being exercised on the
  part of the engager;
- personal service required on behalf of the worker;
- other provisions of the contract being consistent with
  a contract of employment.

A contractor's contract will need to set out a strict schedule
detailing the services they are to provide to the client. They
are under no obligation to undertake any further work
beyond what is contractually agreed. Neither is the client
obliged to offer any work beyond what has already been set
out.

This is critical at it ensures the contractor continues to carry
out project-based work as opposed to role-based work
which would instead be consistent with a contract of
employment.

In one IR35 judgement, the judges cited a statement by the
client manager calling the contractor a 'tail-end Charlie',
meaning that the contractor did whatever other members of
the team didn't complete. Carrying out this sort of work is
powerful evidence of you being treated as an employee,
and will act against you in an IR35 case.

You should show that you have the right to refuse further
work from the client. You are not obliged to turn up at the
client's office every day and just work at what is assigned.
You pick and choose your contracts: you accept one,
perform it, and then choose whether or not to accept
another.

## 5.9 Financial risk

Your exposure to financial risk will be examined if you are required to contest your IR35 status. Employees are protected from any exposure to financial loss, whatever involvement they may have in a given project.

This is not the case for a contractor, who may find a project terminated before completion and who then may not collect the full fee. Exposure of this kind is a key factor in determining IR35 status and it should be clear in any contract that you sign. If you appear to have the same protection as that enjoyed by an employee, HMRC and the judge may consider you one.

You can demonstrate financial risk in many ways. These include:

- Having to invoice for work
- Having to negotiate rates
- Working on a fixed price per project basis
- Being able to profit, for example by finishing a fixed-price contract early
- Making a loss on a project
- Suffering bad debts
- Having to correct mistakes in your own time and at your own cost
- Buying stocks or supplies

A contract that does not show a price for the work and an approximate date for completion implies there is no financial risk. It would simply state that you will work a set number of hours per week for an hourly rate, which is little different from an employment contract.

Many contracts are like this though, so it is advisable to consider including a clause that says for a limited period you will correct mistakes made in your own time and at your own cost. And if a mistake was discovered after you finished the project, and you went back and fixed it for free then this is a good pointer towards your outside IR35 status.

## 5.10 Part and parcel

Want to use the company canteen when you're working on assignment? Want to share car rides with other employees when you go home? Want to get a security pass to avoid the bother of signing in each time? Well, don't even think about it, because even these small things can help to put you inside IR35.

Unfortunately, when you are working on site under contract, you can easily get mistaken for an employee. It can be hard to distinguish what you are doing from what the permanent employees are doing. You can also find yourself being sucked into the employee workforce: eating at the company cafeteria, being added to internal phone directories and organisation charts and even given business cards to use.

Yet another of HMRC's tests of IR35 is whether you are 'part and parcel' of the client's organisation or not. HMRC will contend that the provision of work by a contractor is the same as that of an employee and that the contractor is part and parcel of the end user client's business. In other words, the taxman will see that contractor as an employee, with all the tax implications that brings with it.

In case law there are no clear determinations of what 'part and parcel' means. In fact, some judges don't consider this test a very useful one in determining employment status. But others do, and HMRC certainly use part and parcel as a test of IR35, so you need to be careful in how you manage the relationship with your client.

To make certain that you avoid the attention of HMRC inspectors, simply avoid looking like an employee and don't accept any of the conveniences that employees take for granted:

- Don't accept a pass that lets you into the building through the employee gate; sign-in every day, or use a pass that identifies you as a temporary contractor
- Don't allow yourself to become listed in the company telephone directory
- Don't get your business cards from the company
- Accept no sick pay or holiday pay from the client
- Don't eat at the company canteen
- In so far as possible, see that you're not listed on company materials as part of the organisation

If you have a management role, make it clear in written form that this is strictly related to the project you have contracted for. In general, it is best to avoid written materials that put you in the light of being an employee in any way; this is just what HMRC will be looking for.

Make sure you document some facts to back up your arguments during your current contract in case of an investigation – which could be six years from now and you may have forgotten the details if you haven't added them to your contract file.

Draw up a list of the differences between you as a contractor and the client's employees. As you are not an employee, there should be obvious differences, such as not having set hours, benefits, pension arrangements, access to social clubs, parking, expenses arrangements, use of a subsidised staff canteen and so on.

Try and keep any correspondence with the client that shows clearly you are not under complete control of the client's project manager. Keep this file safe with the relevant financial records from the same period. If HMRC come knocking, you can simply reach out and produce the file. Chapter 8 details setting up and maintaining the right records to support your case if you come under HMRC investigation.

# 5.11 Provision of equipment

This can be a rather tricky test for knowledge based workers, and those working in sectors where they are required to use the client's equipment. For IT contractors in particular, using the client's computers and networks is just a basic requirement of IT security; an IT director would be irresponsible to let hundreds of contractors into the organisation using their own equipment and posing a huge range of risks to mission critical operations.

Unfortunately, several conclusions can be drawn if you use a client's equipment, including that you are taking no financial risk by investing in your own equipment and that you are being slightly controlled by the client. However, if HMRC try to draw negative conclusions about your use of the client's equipment there are actions you can take to counter those conclusions.

You can demonstrate that you are in business in your own right – which might involve you buying equipment that you simply use on the project but it isn't on the client's networks – you are taking financial risks. For example, you may decide to carry out a task using your own equipment that you bring to the client, such as a piece of software that they do not have in house.

# 5.12 Being in business on your own account (IBOYOA)

If you are in business on your own account (IBOYOA), it is a solid indication that you are a legitimate businessperson supplying services via a limited company. Whilst in the grand scheme of things it's a relatively small factor, compared with the likes of control and substitution, demonstrating evidence that you are IBOYOA may help to swing an IR35 judgement in your favour.

There is a range of activities that can demonstrate that you are in business in your own right, rather than a de facto employee. Initially, these activities are likely to take the form of marketing – after all, if you were not in business, why would you market your company?

Simple steps include:

- A company website, business cards and company stationery
- Company social media activity, such as writing a company blog, a company LinkedIn page and a company Twitter account, all of which you keep active
- Advertising on business websites and in trade publications
- Evidence of writing proposals and winning business
- Negotiating higher rates of pay

There is of course a cost associated with each of these activities, but compared with what you would lose if found within IR35, the cost is trivial.

When naming your limited company, avoid using your own name, as this implies you are only providing your own services. If you have Jane Smith Ltd on your business card, the implication is that Jane Smith will be completing the work. If the right of substitution is exercised and John Smith turns up, this might, understandably, cause some confusion.

It is also recommended that you do not use a company name that clearly says you are a contractor, such as IT Contractor Solutions Ltd, as this could also imply that you are the IT contractor, leading to similar confusion.

If, however, you call the company ABC Computing, you are simply providing computing services that could be supplied by anyone from your firm, John or Jane Smith or, indeed, another contractor that you might sub-contract some or all of the work to.

Contractors who can show they have invested in business equipment also demonstrate that they are running a business. Business equipment could include:

- Tablets, laptops, software, peripherals and consumables
- Business telephone, smartphone, fixed-line broadband
- Office equipment, such as a desk, office chair and a filing cabinet
- Business insurances, including professional indemnity, public liability, employee liability and business contents

A library of training material, investment in membership of a professional body, training courses and subscriptions to trade magazines all paid for by your limited company can all be indication that you are in business for yourself. Never charge materials like these back to a client, even if they offer, as it could be used as evidence of you being an employee.

Having concurrent clients can be a strong indication of being in business for yourself, but as evidence it tends to be treated on a case by case basis. For example, if you are earning £75,000 a year doing high end development work for a corporate client, and maybe £5,000 per year producing websites for family and friends, then HMRC would not take this as evidence by itself that you are in business for yourself.

However, if you work two days on one contract for £35,000 per year and three days for £40,000 on another contract for a separate client, then this is strong evidence of genuine concurrent clients.

# 5.13 Chapter summary – key lessons for contractors, agencies and clients

## Contractors

- 'Control', 'right of substitution' and 'mutuality of obligation' are the three key tests of employment which underpin all UK employment status cases.

- To be genuine, a right of substitution must be unfettered. An actual substitution will provide concrete evidence that you are outside IR35.

- It is vital that you ensure your working practices match what is written in the contract, as all available evidence would be considered by a Tax Tribunal judge.

## Agencies

- Contractors will insist on engaging in a *contract for services*, which is different to a contract between employer and employee.

- Helping contractors negotiate changes to their contracts is essential in minimising the risk of IR35 for all parties.

- If you cannot help the contractor stay outside IR35 then they may seek work elsewhere.

## Clients

- IR35 status is based on the true nature of the working arrangements between the contractor and client. Paper contracts must reflect reality.

- If you want to hire a contractor and keep them outside IR35 then you will not be able to treat them like one of your employees.

- A contractor may request that you sign a confirmation of arrangements that provides additional detail that is not in the contract. This helps protect both yourself and the contractor should HMRC decide to investigate.

# 6

# Applying IR35 to public sector contracts

6. Applying IR35 to public sector contracts

# 6.1 What are the changes to IR35 in the public sector?

As of April 2017, reform to how IR35 is enforced in the public sector shifts the compliance burden from the contractor to the public sector client and agency, meaning significant changes for the whole contractor supply chain.

**Public sector IR35 reform – in summary**

- No changes are made to the IR35 rules themselves; just how they are enforced in the public sector,
- The responsibility for checking IR35 status and the associated tax liability are removed from the contractor
- Public sector clients have responsibility for checking IR35 status
- Public sector clients also have responsibility for calculating, processing and paying tax when they directly engage a contractor inside IR35
- Where an agency is involved, they take on the burden of calculating and paying tax, but the client remains responsible for checking IR35 status

HMRC's draft legislation released in December 2016 didn't make it clear which party would assume the tax liability when a contractor who has been paying tax outside IR35 is found to be caught by IR35 – which could be either the client or the agency. However, when a contractor is found to have provided fraudulent evidence to prove that they are outside IR35, they take on liability for any tax, penalties and interest.

**Why has the IR35 reform come about?**

The changes were in response to what HMRC referred to as 'widespread non-compliance with the IR35 legislation'. The taxman estimated that £440m would be lost to non-compliance with IR35 in 2016-17, claiming just 10% of contractors in the whole of the public sector paid the correct tax[1].

From April 2017, if a contractor engaged with a public sector client is found to be caught by IR35, both they and their client will be required to pay broadly the same tax and NICs as if they were an employee. HMRC notes that taxes will be reported through the Real Time Information (RTI) system.

Experts consider HMRC's proposals to be a massive oversimplification of IR35, and have pointed out that its notoriously complicated rules are far beyond the understanding and subsequent application of agencies and public sector clients.

HMRC intends to minimise the burden on engagers and provide more clarity and certainty. This is in the form of an online tool released in time for the introduction of the legislation in April 2017. This tool is called the Employment Status Service (ESS) and takes the form of an online questionnaire. HMRC claims it will provide public sector clients with an answer on the IR35 status of the contractor that they are checking in most cases, and it is understood that HMRC intends for the ESS to deliver either a definitive pass or fail verdict.

1.   HMRC, *Off-payroll working in the public sector: reform of the intermediaries' legislation*

This is in spite of the fact that IR35 is incredibly complex and often subjective. It is steeped in decades of employment case law, and the only way an online tool can present an accurate evaluation of IR35 status is by displaying an individual's risk along a spectrum.

HMRC will not pass a contractor unless it is 100% certain that they are outside IR35, meaning many legitimately outside IR35 contractors will be deemed caught by the ESS which insists upon providing a definite decision, one way or the other. HMRC has also said that it will be bound by any decision determined by the ESS, even though it cannot be legally binding.

**Forcing contractors into inside-IR35 contracts**

Another issue flagged up by experts is that public sector contractors whose working arrangements are legitimately outside of IR35 are likely to be unjustifiably forced into an inside-IR35 contract. This is very likely to arise from reluctance by engagers to accept the risk of additional tax liabilities – be it even a small risk – because they have little or no prior experience or understanding of IR35.

Experts suggested in 2016 that the new rules would be likely to result in a migration of contracting talent away from the public sector, intensifying skills shortages. A survey conducted by ContractorCalculator in July 2016 found that 80% of contractors would sooner abandon the public sector than accept an inside-IR35 contract under the new regime. A separate study by the Association of Independent Professionals and the Self Employed (IPSE) published in August 2016 revealed that 31% of contractors would refuse to work on public sector contracts after the introduction of the reforms, without waiting to find out their IR35 status.

Though HMRC insists that the reforms won't be stretched into the private sector, many experts anticipate that the public sector measures are a 'test-run', expecting a mass roll-out to follow.

**The challenge for contractors**

The threat posed by the reforms is very real, not only to contractors in the public sector, but also agencies, clients and then private sector contractors in a later expected rollout.

The challenge for contractors is to persuade engagers to agree to an outside-IR35 contract and convince them that there is no risk to their organisation. Engagers want to avoid any financial risk, but they need to carry out the necessary compliance work and provide outside-IR35 contracts where suitable to attract contractors.

Contractors are far less likely to consider a client if they only offer contracts inside IR35, and the impact on business could be substantial. This is why engagers must conduct due diligence and ensure that contractors are tested fairly, which will be enough to ensure that the engager avoids any tax risk.

## The dangers of using the Employment Status Service

Many experts who have consulted with HMRC on the IR35 reforms have expressed considerable concern that the ESS doesn't align with the case law that underpins IR35. As a result, the outcome determined by the ESS will be inadvertently biased in HMRC's favour, and will only provide a pass result in a handful of cases. However, that doesn't then imply that only a tiny proportion of contractors are outside IR35.

Due to the subjective nature of IR35, this is very rarely the case. Whilst there are certain factors that alone suggest that a contractor is either definitely inside or outside IR35, other factors would indicate that it's more or less likely that a contractor is caught. As such, IR35 status, or risk, can only really be accurately displayed along a spectrum. However, it is currently understood that the ESS only delivers one of two decisions – pass or fail. Naturally, HMRC will only provide a pass result where it is 100% sure that the contractor is outside IR35. This is very rarely the case.

Consequently, experts have warned that use of the ESS by clients as a means of conducting due diligence could see thousands of legitimate contractors forced into inside-IR35 contracts by an inaccurate judgement. The ESS promises to provide certainty with its judgement, but that isn't to say it will always reflect reality.

Engagers need to be made aware that there are other, more considered means of demonstrating due diligence that will give the contractor a greater chance of securing an outside-IR35 contract. Encouraging a contractor to undergo an independent contract review is one. Another is using alternative independent online solutions, such as ir35testing.co.uk, the most comprehensive and accurate online IR35 test available.

## 6.2 How the public sector IR35 rules differ

There are no differences between the public and private sector as to what factors determine a contractor's employment status, and the existing employment status tests are still appropriate. For the key factors impacting IR35 status, see chapter 5. The significant difference is in the enforcement and application of IR35.

Prior to April 2017, all contractors are required to determine whether the rules apply to a contract by examining the underlying relationship between themselves and their client. If they fall within IR35 they should either pay themselves all their fees as salary, or make a deemed payment calculation of their tax liabilities at the end of the year, although accountants advise the former as it is a much simpler process.

### Compliance burden shifts

However, from April 2017 for contractors in the public sector, the new rules shift the responsibility for determining whether IR35 rules apply from the contractor to the public sector client. HMRC has yet to confirm who will be liable for unpaid tax, penalties and interest if HMRC investigates and judges that a contractor who has been processed as outside IR35 is caught. However, it is expected that the liability will fall with either the client or the agency if there is one.

In most public sector based contractual chains, a contractor's limited company will source work with a client via a recruitment agency, in which case the agency will assume responsibility for calculating, processing and paying tax, as instructed by the client. If the contractor were to contract direct with the public sector client, the client would be responsible for deducting tax. Where there are several agencies in a contractual chain, the agency that contracts directly with the contractor's limited company assumes responsibility. In the draft legislation they are referred to as the "fee payer".

Where it is determined that the contractor has fraudulently provided the engager with incorrect information to avoid being caught by IR35, the contractor themselves will be personally liable for any outstanding tax and NICs.

## Concerns over HMRC's Employment Status Service

Most public sector bodies have had no experience of complying with IR35, which is why HMRC has attempted to simplify the process with its ESS tool. The taxman claims its tool, an online employment status questionnaire, can provide upfront certainty in any contractor's particular situation.

However, a definite IR35 conclusion cannot always be drawn from completing a questionnaire. The use of any online tool needs to be considered as a part of a more comprehensive due diligence process, prior to obtaining a contract review from an IR35 expert. Contractors need to make their clients well aware of this, or risk being unjustly bundled into an inside-IR35 contract by way of an incorrect judgement.

## 6.3 How will the changes impact the public sector?

**The impact on recruitment agencies**

Agencies are responsible for calculating, reporting and paying each contractor's tax via RTI when the contractor is judged to be inside IR35 by the client. This brings with it further operating costs. Many agencies will also incur the initial one-time cost of merging systems to comply with the taxman's processing requirements. It is expected that most agencies will outsource this burden, although it will come at a cost that some may seek to counteract by increasing their margins.

It means that agencies are also required to make employer's NI contributions for each contractor caught by IR35. This looks set to become a substantial cost for agencies that operate modest margins, with experts predicting that many will be forced to increase their margins, in turn increasing the cost along the whole supply chain. This could inadvertently benefit public sector contractors, with agencies more inclined to help contractors negotiate outside-IR35 contracts.

**The impact on public sector clients**

HMRC has confirmed that the public sector client will always be responsible for checking the contractor's IR35 status, even where an agency is involved. We do not know for sure who will be liable for unpaid tax, penalties and interest in the instance of an incorrect IR35 judgement. Unless the contractor has provided fraudulent information, it is expected that it will either be the client or the agency.

HMRC is strongly encouraging clients to use its ESS tool to determine IR35 status and has claimed it will be bound by any decision it makes. Clients may see it as a risk-free solution and, with no in-house staff with sufficient knowledge to ensure correct compliance procedures are followed, will be very tempted to use it.

However, tax experts and contractors are well aware of the inadequacies of the tool, and know that its shortcomings will make the contractor appear to be inside IR35 in many cases where they are not. As a result, the majority of contractors will be reluctant to engage with clients who rely on the ESS and determine that they are inside IR35, and will instead insist that they conduct their due diligence correctly.

Clients who opt to rely solely on the ESS will eliminate risk from a tax and penalty perspective, but they become a markedly less attractive proposition for contractors. In skill-deprived sectors, this poses a significant threat to the ongoing operations of many organisations.

Contractors who do accept inside-IR35 contracts are expected to demand an increase in their rates to account for the tax lost by roughly 20%. Consequently, overall costs for clients will soar. The best course of action for public sector clients is to cooperate with contractors and agencies to carry out due diligence and give each contractor a fair evaluation. This way they can continue to attract contractors, will not be charged premium contract rates and can still minimise their risk of incurring tax and penalties.

**The impact on contractors**

The public sector reforms pose a serious threat to contractors who face a reduction in take-home pay of up to 20% if they cannot get the client and agency on side to conduct proper IR35 compliance.

One positive to come out of the changes for public sector contractors is that they are no longer liable for backdated tax and penalties if they operate an outside IR35 contract which is subsequently challenged and beaten by HMRC. However, the shift in this liability looks likely to cause the biggest hurdle for contractors to overcome in securing an outside IR35 contract.

With clients taking over responsibility for checking IR35 status, and with the liability for tax and penalties expected to fall with either the client or agency, the onus is on contractors to persuade clients and agencies not to adopt a risk-averse approach. This could prove tricky as the fact that very few clients will have IR35 expertise in-house will strengthen the inclination to use the ESS tool that the taxman has vowed it will stick by.

The alternative option for contractors is increasing their rates to compensate for the loss in net earnings. Contractors could price themselves out of a contract, and may be forced to look at the private sector.

A survey conducted by ContractorCalculator in July 2016 found that 80% of contractors said they would turn down an inside-IR35 contract and seek private sector opportunities. This would leave a seriously depleted talent pool for public sector organisations to choose from, but it remains to be seen whether there are enough private sector opportunities to go around.

Agencies will also want to ensure that contractors are offered outside-IR35 contracts, to reduce their own costs. Contractors must be able to assure inexperienced clients and agencies that, by operating the correct compliance procedures, they will be able to engage contractors with minimal tax risk.

## 6.4 Getting an outside-IR35 contract with reluctant engagers

If you're a contractor working in the public sector, the greatest concern is that agencies and clients will refuse to engage with you unless you agree to be taxed as inside-IR35 via RTI, without receiving any employment rights.

Very few clients and agencies have sufficient IR35 expertise in-house to be anything other than risk averse. But there are many ways to persuade an engager to give you a fair assessment and help guarantee that you aren't taxed excessively.

**Review your contract independently before signing**

Securing an independent evaluation of your contract not only demonstrates your due diligence but it could be enough to assure all parties that your contract is outside IR35. The first step is to check the status of your contract online. Rather than using HMRC's ESS tool, which does not align closely with case law, you should seek out an alternative independent testing solution.

The best of these is ir35testing.co.uk. Following a quick questionnaire, this comprehensive solution will display your IR35 risk on a spectrum, allowing you to make an informed decision regarding your next move.

This should probably be to get your contract professionally reviewed. With the inexperience and uncertainty of the client being the barrier between you and an outside IR35 contract, who better to provide reassurance than a legal expert who can confirm your employment status with confidence? Passing a contract review before signing a contract should lay to rest any doubts that your client may have that your contract is outside IR35.

However, you must choose an IR35 specialist who has the following:

- Employment law expertise
- Proven expertise and track record in evaluating IR35 contract risks
- Specific experience in the contract sector, with contractor, agency and end-user client customers

Do not use HMRC's contract review service. Using this service suggests that you are doubtful about your status and is an open invitation for HMRC to come and investigate you. Using the ESS service developed by the taxman will almost certainly find you inside IR35.

## Negotiate terms with the client and agency

After assessing your IR35 status both online and by way of securing an expert contract review, you'll know exactly what amendments need to be made to your contract to minimise any risk that HMRC will target you for IR35. Present the feedback gathered from your earlier due diligence to your agency and client and explain the changes that need to be made. Ideally, you'll want to involve the IR35 expert who carried out your contract review in this process. This is both to reassure the client and agency that the negotiated amends are necessary and legitimate, and to ensure that any changes are correct and don't deviate from what is expected.

You should reinforce that any amendments won't result in any significant changes to the contract itself, and are all typical of a limited company contractor's contract. Fortunately, negotiating contractual changes in the public sector shouldn't prove too difficult. Your agency has an incentive to ensure you remain outside IR35 as it will incur the administrative burden of calculating, reporting and paying your tax if you are found inside IR35, as well as having to make employer's NI contributions.

Logically, clients should also be keen to do all they can to keep you outside IR35. This is because, should a contractor be deemed inside IR35 where a client has been uncooperative, the likely outcome is they will increase their rate in order to retain the same net pay. However, there is the concern that the fear of incurring tax liability could act as a deterrent from offering outside-IR35 contracts.

**Get a confirmation of arrangements**

Whilst conducting a professional IR35 contract review and negotiating your contract to be a contract of services should provide all the assurance you need to stay outside IR35, the tax liability that the client or agency is set to assume may mean they want further certainty before committing. Getting a confirmation of arrangements letter for the client to sign off is a simple and effective solution for all parties involved.

This will describe the working relationship in more detail than the contract itself and can be used as part of a compliance file should HMRC come knocking. Amongst other indicators that your contract is outside IR35, your confirmation of arrangements will highlight:

- That the client exerts no control over how you carry out your work
- That you have an unfettered right of substitution that the client is aware of
- That you will not take on work not specified in the contract

However, you'll need to ensure that all details included in the confirmation of arrangements letter align with your actual working practices. Because of this, it's advisable to get an IR35 expert involved in the process. This will also help to reassure the client.

A simple alternative is to get the client to sign the sign off sheet included with the IR35 report available to purchase from ir35testing.co.uk. This is a simple means of confirming your working arrangements as it will reaffirm your status as indicated by your test results. This can prove very useful and is another way to bulk up your body of evidence ready for the taxman, offering further protection to your client.

**Negotiate rights or higher rates with an inside-IR35 contract**

Policymakers may have failed to realise this but it's wholly unfair for a contractor to be taxed as an employee without receiving the rights that accompany employment. If your client continues to insist that they will not grant you the outside IR35 contract that your working arrangements warrant, it may be time to turn the tables.

For example, you may suggest that if they want to tax you as an employee they should place you on a fixed-term employment contract. This would grant you:

- The same pay and conditions as permanent staff
- The same or equivalent benefits package
- Protection against redundancy or dismissal

Alternatively, if the client doesn't want to hire you with these elements in place, you may wish to increase your rate to compensate for the deduction in take-home pay you're set to suffer. This tactic is expected to be used by many contractors who will bump up their rates by roughly 20% to receive the same net income as they would have outside IR35. Just make sure you don't price yourself out of the market.

# 6.5 Chapter summary – key lessons for contractors, agencies and clients

## Contractors

- No changes are being made to the IR35 legislation in itself, only the manner in which it is enforced in the public sector.

- When dealing with agencies and clients who have little, if any, prior experience of IR35, you are strongly advised to seek help from qualified IR35 experts.

- You should not use HMRC's ESS tool to determine your IR35 status as it is likely to fail you even if you are outside IR35.

## Agencies

- The public sector reforms instruct that agencies deduct tax at source for contractors deemed to be within IR35.

- If you're an agency engaging public sector contractors, you will need to work very closely with both the contractor, the client and IR35 experts to ensure contracts and working arrangements put your contractors very clearly outside of IR35.

- Contractors who cannot be offered inside IR35 contracts are expected to increase their rates by 20% or avoid the public sector entirely. Therefore securing an outside-IR35 contracts for each contractor is critical.

**Clients**

- The responsibility for checking a public sector contractor's IR35 status falls with the client from April 2017.

- The cost of sourcing talent is expected to rise for public sector clients as a result of the changes, with agencies and contractors likely to increase margins and fees respectively to account for greater operating costs and lost earnings.

- Contractors are unlikely to engage with public sector clients who assess their contract as inside IR35. It is essential you seek expert IR35 advice to attract and retain contract resources.

# 7

# Special IR35 rules for office holders

# 7.1 Office holders can be caught by IR35

Contractors who are fulfilling the duties of an office holder for a client may also be automatically caught by IR35. This is as a result of legislation introduced in April 2013 that withdrew an exemption from the intermediaries legislation that office holders held. Prior to its introduction, contractors in office holding roles had to pay National Insurance Contributions (NICs) but weren't subject to different tax treatment. However, unlike typical contractors, office holders undergo a reduced set of tests to determine their IR35 status.

# 7.2 What is an office holder?

Although there is no statutory definition of the word 'office', the judicial definition of an office holder, highlighted in Section 5 of the Income Tax (Earnings and Pensions) Act 2003, states that said individual fulfils a:

*'permanent, substantive position which had an existence independent from the person who filled it, which went on and was filled in succession by successive holders.'*

This is relevant to contractors as some may assume senior roles within their client's organisation, many of which will fulfil the 'office holder' criteria. These include:

- Chairman
- Director
- Non-executive director
- Nominee director
- Roles such as 'Treasurer'

**Office holding roles bring IR35 threat**

Positions likely to fall into the category of an office holder, as defined by case law and understood by HMRC, are more prevalent in the public sector than the private sector as many public sector offices are created by statute. Therefore, contractors on assignments requiring them to occupy a role that is perceived to be office holding need to beware that they are at greater risk of being caught by IR35.

Contractors who are offered any such role at a client's organisation should also understand the IR35 risk that the position creates and the necessary practices that must be undertaken to test their status.

For example, you may be appointed into a financial director's role that was previously held by a succession of employees, has been a long standing role in your client's organisation and will be for years to come. This suggests that you have become an office holder and must operate IR35.

**Office holding – what it is and what it isn't**

However, just because a title sounds like an office holding role doesn't make it necessarily so. In the House of Lords decision in Edwards v Clinch (1981), Lord Wilberforce determined that for a role to be office holding it must involve a degree of continuance and of independent existence, concluding that it must mean or imply:

*'a post to which a person can be appointed, which he can vacate and to which a successor can be appointed.'*

It is for this reason that contractor positions such as interim manager does not fall within the remit of office holding. Because it is a temporary position, there is no possibility of it being succeeded by anyone else once the contractor has completed the contract.

# 7.3 Office holders and personal service

Unusually, when considering the IR35 status of a contractor in an office holding role, two of the three tests of employment – control and mutuality of obligation – are not relevant. Similarly, other factors that are considered in a typical IR35 investigation, such as being in business on your own account, part and parcel and financial risk, do not apply.

This is because the tax legislation now found in Section 5 of the ITEPA 2003 was designed to follow the existing NIC legislation at the time, which contained narrower testing requirements than those currently applied to IR35.

Instead, the only test of employment you need to consider when assessing your status is whether or not personal service is required, or whether you have an 'unfettered right of substitution (see section 5.7).

If your contract states that you have the right to draft in a replacement to provide the services agreed in your contract, and your client cannot reserve the right to stop you from sending in a substitute, the likelihood of you being caught by IR35 is very slim.

**Office holding roles often require personal service**

This may make it appear as if it's a lot easier to prove you are outside IR35 in an office holding role, but more often than not that simply isn't the case. Contractors are generally appointed to office holding roles specifically for the individual skills and experience they bring. Therefore, it is highly unusual for a client to accept and confirm to HMRC that the contractor's personal service isn't required.

It is critical that you seek professional advice from an IR35 expert should you be offered a role that you believe could be an 'office'. Otherwise you leave yourself at greater risk of IR35 than you would in a regular contract role without carrying out IR35 best practice.

## Proving your position is not office holding

Alternatively, you may seek to prove that your position is not an office holder. Case law elaborates on the judicial definition of an office holder, adding that an office:

*'... must owe its existence to some constituent instrument, whether it be a charter, statute, declaration of trust, contract (other than a contract of personal service) or instrument of some other kind.'*

Building on the judicial definition of an 'office' which highlights that the position must have had an existence independent from the person who filled it, experts have suggested that certain less typical roles such as 'chief executive officer' and 'programme director' may not be classed as office holding.

This is because they will not generally be positions that exist according to a charter or statute. It may well be that the role you assume is not an office role as defined by case law, although as highlighted above it's always best to seek expert advice.

# 7.4 Chapter summary – key lessons for contractors, agencies and clients

## Contractors

- Only the employment test of personal service is considered when determining whether a contractor in an office holding role is caught by IR35.

- The tax legislation regarding office holding rules has narrower testing requirements than those currently applied to IR35.

- Contractors are generally appointed to office holding roles specifically for their individual skills and experience, implying personal service.

## Agencies

- Contractors who accept office holding roles, such as chairman or treasurer, are likely to be caught by IR35.

- If you're an agency engaging public sector contractors, you will need to inform your clients of the risks associated with office holding roles.

- If a contractor has a right of substitution in place with regards to their fulfilment of their office holding role, they are at little risk of IR35, though this is a rare scenario.

## Clients

- Assigning a contractor an office holding role, such as financial director, places them at immediate risk of being caught by IR35.

- Public sector clients, who are responsible for determining the IR35 status of contractors, should carry out reassessments of their contractors.

- Temporary roles such as interim manager don't count as office holding, because the position itself is temporary and so a successor cannot be appointed once the contractor has completed the contract.

# 8

# Ensuring IR35 doesn't affect you

8. Ensuring IR35 doesn't affect you

# 8.1 The dangers of IR35

The best IR35 defence begins before an investigation even starts and, ideally, before you sign a contract. If you invest time in engineering out the risk of IR35, it is likely to save you huge sums of money and ensure any future HMRC challenge is quickly overcome and closed down.

This section is not about pretending to be in business for yourself if you are not. If your contract and working conditions put you inside IR35 and there is no scope of changing that fact then you must pay tax as an employee; it's as clear-cut as that.

This section is about making sure that in your legitimate work as a contractor running a limited company there can be no room for suspicion by HMRC or a judge that you are a disguised employee and therefore caught by IR35.

**Stay off HMRC's radar**

The most effective strategy is not to attract HMRC's attention in the first place. Guaranteeing that you don't do anything that will result in your company or you personally getting on the taxman's radar, such as filing late or incorrect tax returns, significantly reduces your chances of being targeted for investigation.

If your efforts to stay off HMRC's radar fail and you find that you are challenged by the taxman, having all your defence paperwork and other evidence prepared and filed will leave you well equipped to close down the investigation before it's even started. If you've prepared well, the tax inspector is likely to look into your case, quickly conclude that you're acting in full accordance with the law, and move on to easier targets.

The other key fact to consider is that an investigation can go back six years, or even more if HMRC suspects fraud, even if your company has since been closed down. Can you remember exactly what you were doing on every contract all those years ago? Will your client be able to remember? Collecting and keeping records as you go means that you won't have to scramble to prepare a defence when it may be too late.

## 8.2 Steps to avoiding IR35

### Step 1 - Don't rush into signing a contract

Firstly, under no circumstances should you sign a contract without being fully aware of the IR35 implications. Remember, an inside IR35 contract can mean a decrease of up to 20% of your take home pay, so don't commit to anything without knowing all the details. Never accept assurances from agencies or clients that you are outside IR35. Unless you are working for a public sector client, agencies generally aren't interested in your IR35 status – they get paid the same regardless.

Agencies aren't experts in employment law, and even if you are convinced they are giving you correct advice, it cannot be relied upon in a legal defence. As such, you would be wise to conduct your own due diligence, detailed later in this chapter. Otherwise, you could find yourself in court saying something the equivalent of, "Some bloke called Bob told me it was alright." The judge might find it amusing, but it certainly won't help your case.

### Step 2 - Test your IR35 status online

Checking your IR35 status using an online tool is an important first step in conducting your due diligence, and informs and prepares you prior to undergoing an IR35 review, which is the next potential step.

ir35testing.co.uk is a free-to-use solution that is frequently updated to align with the latest tax tribunal outcomes and employment case law precedents that underpin IR35, making it the most accurate test on the market. The test presents your level of IR35 risk on a spectrum, and provides access to information detailing how you can further reduce your risk of being caught by IR35.

## Step 3 - Get your contract reviewed by an expert

An IR35 expert can review your status and give you an accurate assessment based on your situation. This is all for a relatively small fee when considering the tax savings you'll be making with an outside IR35 contract.

Asking an IR35 specialist to review your contracts provides solid proof that you are conducting your due diligence. A contract review from a contracts lawyer would also be wise if there are commercial factors you wish to have considered professionally. This assessment, along with other testimony and materials, can also be useful to you if HMRC comes knocking at your door.

## Step 4 - Negotiate changes into your contract

Having your contract reviewed by an IR35 expert will inform you of any necessary changes that need to be made to your contract to keep you IR35 compliant. With the written contract being the first port of call for any HMRC inspector, it's important that you are able to amend these details.

Traditionally, it has been of little interest to the agency or client to negotiate changes into a contract as there is little benefit to them. However, if market conditions are favourable, and the agency has no other contractors to place, you may find that they are more receptive to your requests.

## Step 5 - Sign a confirmation of arrangements

A confirmation of arrangements is a written statement that describes the working relationship in greater detail than the contract itself, highlighting the numerous aspects that indicate that the contract is outside IR35. For example, a typical confirmation of arrangements would note that the client doesn't instruct you on how to complete your work, and that you can provide a substitute at your expense, should you wish. Having a client sign this will form a critical part of your defence should HMRC ever challenge your status.

Alternatively, if you choose to test your IR35 status online with ir35testing.co.uk, you can purchase a status report which includes a sign off sheet for the client to sign to confirm your working arrangements. This can prove very useful and will bulk up your body of evidence ready for the taxman.

**Step 6 - Adhere to the contract and build a compliance file**

After securing an outside-IR35 contract, always adhere to it with your day-to-day working practices and document how you have done so to protect yourself should HMRC come knocking at a later date.

The IR35 decision determined by HMRC and tax tribunal judges will be based on the notional contract. This is the real life day-to-day working relationship between the contractor and client, gauged from the written contracts and other supplementary evidence.

This makes it all the more important that you create a compliance file for every contract, containing every piece of useful proof you can get. Keep all the paperwork and/or electronic files throughout your contracting career. Should HMRC investigate you and suspect fraud, it can trace your contracting history as far back as 20 years.

## 8.3 Evaluating your status using online tools and experts

HMRC requires that all taxpayers demonstrate reasonable care in the management of their tax affairs. However, the taxman fails to provide a definition of what reasonable care entails. Experts advise that conducting due diligence to evaluate and understand your IR35 position by way of using online IR35 tests and securing IR35 reviews demonstrates this.

The first key fact to remember about contract reviews is to get the contract reviewed before you sign it. If you have it looked at after you have signed it, and there are IR35 issues, you've missed your chance to renegotiate. The agency will simply say it's too late and there will be nothing you can do about it.

**Evaluating your status online**

Prior to obtaining a contract review, it's important to evaluate your status using an online tool. After all, there's no point in spending money on a contract review if it turns out you had no chance of passing IR35 in the first place.

The main independent IR35 testing solution available is ir35testing.co.uk, which is free-to-use and can provide an accurate evaluation of your IR35 status within minutes. This is a necessary first step to ensuring you attain an outside IR35 contract compliantly, and an extremely simple one.

The benefits to using an online tool to evaluate your IR35 status include:

- You can accurately determine your IR35 risk and decide whether or not to proceed with an IR35 review
- Any report provided can be used to demonstrate due diligence to HMRC at a later date if required

- You can identify risk factors impacting your status and receive guidance on how to mitigate them

As well as providing a case law-backed assessment of your IR35 status, an online solution like ir35testing.co.uk will often provide extensive guidance on how to overcome any issues it identifies for your specific case. With ir35testing.co.uk all you have to do is complete a simple questionnaire about your contract to receive your evaluation, and your level of IR35 risk will be displayed on a spectrum along with compliance advice. This will help you to make an informed decision on your next move, which in some cases will be to undergo a professional IR35 contract review.

## Securing a professional contract review

When reviewing a contract for a new assignment you have four options:

1. Don't review your contract (a horrifyingly common approach)
2. Review the contract yourself
3. Get the contract reviewed by an IR35 specialist
4. Ask HMRC to review your contract for you.

Choosing not to review your contract leaves you at risk and may cost you a large amount of money in the long run as a result of claims for back taxes, interest and IR35 penalties by HMRC. The contract may be within IR35, you may get investigated and you will have collected no factual evidence to support a defence. Remember that HMRC has six years to review your contract itself, and can go back even further if it suspects fraud.

It is possible for some highly experienced contractors with a solid understanding of contract law and employment law to self-evaluate their contract. However, this is not recommended, as a self-review may not warrant 'reasonable care' in HMRC's eyes.

Remember, most contractors are not lawyers. Using an online IR35 test is always the best first port of call. Beyond providing you with an accurate assessment, it will recommend that you secure a contract review if your result is not a clear pass.

When you get your contract reviewed by a specialist, make sure:

- You are using an IR35 specialist and not a high street solicitor or non-specialised accountant, because IR35 is a niche topic requiring employment legislation expertise.
- The IR35 specialist you use has expertise and a track record in evaluating IR35 contract risks, preferably with litigation and/or litigation support experience. Very few high street solicitors and accountants will have this combination of expertise
- The specialist has experience specific to the contractor sector, with past and existing contractor, agency and end-user client customers
- You should get the non-IR35 elements of the contract reviewed by a professional adviser who is expert in contract law. Ex-HMRC inspectors are an excellent source of expert IR35 assistance, but they are not contract law experts.

**Beware of HMRC's Employment Status Service**

It is very strongly recommended that you steer clear of HMRC's Employment Status Service (ESS) tool, as its outcome is inadvertently skewed towards providing contractors with a fail result. This is in large part down to the fact that it is based on the taxman's own interpretation of how IR35 should apply, and not the employment case law that underpins the legislation.

HMRC insists that the ESS tool provides upfront certainty regarding IR35 status in almost every instance – which let's face it, is easy to do if you simply fail anyone you are unsure about. But, actual proper certainty simply cannot be achieved in reality if aligning to all of the case law. The only way to conclusively determine a contractor's IR35 status is to have an experienced status expert examine their contract and working arrangements in a level of detail beyond the capabilities of an online tool. There are just too many marginal cases and details that will be specific to the contract that a more generalised tool simply won't be able to cover.

IR35 is subjective by nature, and whilst answers to certain questions alone will suggest a contractor has either definitely passed or failed IR35, others will indicate that it is more or less likely that a contractor has passed. As such, the only way an online test can accurately represent a contractor's status is by presenting it on a spectrum. ir35testing.co.uk does exactly this for you.

The HMRC ESS tool is currently understood to only display two outcomes – pass or fail – meaning it is unable to provide a realistic representation of a contractor's status, and we haven't even got onto the effects of the taxman's conflicting agendas yet.

Naturally, tax collection is HMRC's main priority, meaning it won't want to hand out a pass to any contractor whose result it isn't absolutely sure of. In reality this level of certainty is extremely rare, due to the subjective nature of IR35. But that does mean that only a few contractors actually get a pass result with the ESS tool.

The problem with using the ESS tool is it will only issue a pass in a relative handful of instances, and in the process denying mass amounts of contractors the outside IR35 status that their contract warrants. As a result, you should avoid it at all costs, and instead stick to independent IR35 solutions that not only provide an accurate evaluation of your status, but which also advise on how to fix identified problems and stay outside IR35. It's the old adage – don't ask a barber if you need a haircut!

## Steer clear of HMRC's contract review service

It is also recommended that you do not use HMRC's contract review service. To do so is like waving a flag saying, 'Please come and investigate me!' Plus, if HMRC is asked if there is any doubt about IR35 status, they will always err on the side of caution as they can only tell you that you have passed if they are absolutely sure. This may require you to have carried out a substitution. Never expect an easy ride from HMRC. It's not in the taxman's best interests to help you pass IR35, which is exactly what an independent IR35 expert will do.

Even if you have not reviewed and evaluated contracts for IR35 status in the past, it is a valuable exercise to review them now, so you can accurately plan for any tax implications and structure your payments and tax savings accordingly.

In many cases, your IR35 contract specialist will confirm that your contract is outside IR35. If the contract review uncovers any issues, your IR35 specialist will negotiate with the agency or client in most instances. Occasionally they may provide you with a list containing each element of the contract that needs to be changed and leave you to your own devices.

If the agency or client decides to play hardball over contract negotiations, yet the contract is clearly outside IR35, there are other strategies available to prove your status, which we will discuss further in this chapter.

## 8.4 Negotiating IR35 compliance with agents and clients

Whilst you should focus on your working practices to help your IR35 compliance, a contract is the starting point for an HMRC inspector. If there are IR35-unfriendly features, the taxman will seize on these to direct the initial course of the investigation. Don't give HMRC any ammunition. Ensure what's written down on paper is consistent with your working practices and doesn't place you at risk of being caught by the legislation right from the start.

The agency gets paid the same whether or not you are inside IR35. And it is generally in their interests to get you to sign the contract as quickly as possible, so that they can start taking their cut and then move on to placing another contractor and making more sales.

### Why have agencies and clients been less cooperative in the past?

Traditionally, agencies have sought to avoid the cost and associated risks of amending each and every contract. There are a number of reasons for this. For example, should something go wrong, the client can sue the agency and so the agency will want to reduce their liability. Prior to the public sector reforms, it has rarely been of interest to the client whether the contractor is outside IR35 or not. However, if market conditions favour the contractor, and the agency has nobody else that they can place, the contractor stands a far better chance of negotiating changes to their contract.

With experts predicting that the private sector will follow the public sector and have the same reforms applied, it may well be that all three parties will be working together to ensure contractors can remain contracting outside of IR35. By enacting these measures across the whole sector,

HMRC could inadvertently kill off IR35 all by themselves because any challenge will then become three against one.

Either way, whilst all parties may be keen to ensure compliance and keep their contractors outside of IR35, neither will have the necessary expertise. It's important to ensure you have had expert help during the contract negotiation. This means preparing a list with your IR35 expert of the changes you require, down to the specific wording. Also make it easy for the agent by preparing clauses in bite-sized chunks that integrate seamlessly with the original contract. And if you can, get a more comprehensive confirmation of arrangements signed by the client.

**Public sector changes offer boost to contractors**

Agencies in the public sector will be much more inclined to help you negotiate IR35 compliance. The public sector reforms mean agencies are to assume responsibility for calculating, reporting and paying tax and NICs where a contractor is considered to be inside IR35, as well as paying employer's NI on each invoice. The avoidance of both the administrative burden and the fiscal impact of making NI payments are all the motivation agencies need to help ensure that your contract stays outside IR35.

Being the party responsible for IR35 status checking as of April 2017, clients in the public sector are the ones you'll really need to persuade. Fortunately, clients also have an incentive to negotiate IR35 compliance with you. The public sector reforms may be bad news for contractors, but that isn't to say they will all be bundled into inside-IR35 contracts without a second thought.

Contractors play an intrinsic part in the operation of many public sector services and clients are well aware of the value they add. They are also well aware that very few contractors are willing to settle for an inside-IR35 contract when the means of judgement is dubious. In order to ensure they continue to attract contractors, clients will need to work with them to help keep them outside IR35. The alternative is increased rates across the board from contractors seeking to retain the same net pay. Inevitably, this creates further costs for public sector clients which they will be keen to avoid.

## Employment rights claim could prove useful bargaining tool

One potential way to secure the client's cooperation may be to use the threat of an employment rights claim. Accepting an inside-IR35 contract could provide the contractor with the grounds for an employment rights claim if it can be proven that an implied employment contract exists. This may encourage the client to negotiate an outside-IR35 contract as otherwise the contract would prove more costly for them.

Be warned though, there is uncertainty over how this tactic would pan out, and court cases over the years have yielded mixed results. In the Court of Appeal case Cable & Wireless v Muscat [2006] found that contractor Mr Muscat was an employee of his client Cable & Wireless and therefore warranted employment rights. However, the Court of Appeal case James v Greenwich [2008] determined that it is not usually necessary to imply a contract with a client where an agency contract exists and accurately reflects the working arrangements.

So your chances of securing employment rights in a court settlement may be slim, but the uncertainty over the matter may be enough to convince the client that the risk isn't worth it and that they should negotiate the necessary changes.

## EAT case – Williams v Hewlett Packard

But would you even want to win an employment rights claim? In the EAT case of Williams v Hewlett Packard [2002], limited company contractor John Williams challenged client Hewlett Packard on the basis that he was employed and should receive employment rights after the client unfairly dismissed him. His view was that if the court decided he was not an employee of Hewlett Packard then he would be able to use that fact in any future IR35 defence should HMRC come knocking – which they did.

In the EAT the judge ruled that the provisions of the contract overruled the reality of the engagement, determining that Williams was not an employee of the client. Following the judgement, HMRC chose not to proceed with an intended IR35 investigation of Williams, as the failed employment rights claim served as sufficient evidence that he was outside IR35. Therefore it stands to reason that this tactic could also work for you.

Rather than fighting HMRC, challenging the client and leveraging their legal power could provide you the protection you need without having to pay for it. Remember, the client will be paying lawyers to form all the arguments that you will actually want to use against HMRC. And if your defence is weak and you lose the case, it will mean you are not an employee, and therefore IR35 cannot possibly apply. Granted, you would ruin the relationship with your client in this instance, but if they are already an existing public sector client insisting you are now inside IR35 then hinting to them that this is a route you will consider might make them reconsider their inside/outside decision.

## Termination clauses that avoid IR35 risk

Termination clauses and notice periods vary considerably from contract to contract, but could be an important factor ensuring that you stay outside IR35. Most are designed to protect the client from the sudden departure of a contractor mid-contract.

But termination clauses can also provide a tax tribunal or court with insights into the level of mutuality of obligation between you and your client, helping to determine your IR35 status. Wherever possible, termination clauses should only be included to cover the most serious contract breaches, such as where a contractor makes a serious and costly error or is giving away trade secrets.

From an IR35 perspective, the best kind of termination clause is one that doesn't exist, so that there is no notice period either way. But that may be an unrealistic scenario, particularly as most clients will insist on a termination clause, so that they can quickly shed contractors if a project is cancelled or completed early.

If a project ends naturally ahead of schedule and you stay on because the termination clause says there are four weeks left to run, it is likely the client will be finding you new things to do, and that points strongly towards mutuality of obligation. If there is no notice period it is indicative of being in business and, when viewed with the rest of the evidence, not having that notice period could tip the decision of a tribunal judge in your favour.

## 8.5 Confirming working arrangements with your client

Whilst negotiating an IR35 compliant contract is very important to ensuring you stay outside IR35, it isn't the be-all and end-all of IR35 compliance. IR35 also depends heavily on the ongoing working arrangements between the contractor and client, some of which cannot be captured within a written contract.

For example, the element of control is arguably one of the most important factors when considering a contractor's

IR35 position. Whilst a contract may stipulate, for example, that a contractor can carry out work outside of the client's premises and that they can complete the work during their own working hours, other elements of control need to be evaluated in practice.

This reveals the true nature of the working relationship between the contractor and client that HMRC and, at a later stage, a judge, will consider when making an IR35 status decision, helping them to form what is known as the 'notional contract'.

## Beware of the upper level contract

You must also be warned that upper level contracts between the agent and the client can contradict lower level contracts between the contractor and the agent. HMRC use these contradictions against contractors, even though contractors cannot possibly have any knowledge of the exact contents of these documents.

It is therefore very important that as much evidence as possible is available for each contract demonstrating the true nature of your working relationship. This will considerably strengthen any IR35 defence.

## Get a confirmation of arrangements

One strategy that contractors can employ in a number of circumstances is the confirmation of arrangements letter with the client. This is a document that outlines the working practices of the contractor, confirms there is no control and that the client is aware that the contractor has an unfettered right of substitution, together with many more essential clarifications to prove you are outside IR35. It is also a key step towards ensuring the client understands that their relationship with you is not one of manager and employee.

Your client sets the specifications and expectations of the work to be completed, but that's where their controlling input should end. From the outset, you should make it clear that you are the skilled professional or knowledge worker whose business has been contracted to complete a specific project. As such, you are not subject to supervision, although it is of course acceptable that the client checks the work has been completed to their satisfaction and within agreed deadlines.

## Managing the client's expectations

Furthermore, the covering letter, or email, that accompanies the confirmation of arrangements to be signed by your client provides you with an opportunity to manage the client's expectations about the working relationship they are about to embark upon. This is also an early indication to warn the client of the consequences of deviating from the confirmation of arrangements.

The objective is for the client to sign and date the letter, so if you are asked by HMRC in the future the exact nature of the relationship you had with your client on a given contract, you have written evidence to back up your claims.

Although the letter confirming arrangements should remain valid as long as the original contract is in force, if the project manager at the client changes it is important to ensure they understand the situation, as they may well be giving evidence at your hearing if you get investigated.

Where HMRC tries to use a contradictory upper level contract against you, you can use the notional contract in your favour in this context by producing the confirmation of arrangements that clearly proves the true nature of the relationship. It also provides you with a useful summary that you can keep in your compliance file that will still be valid in many years' time should HMRC decide to investigate you.

**Seek professional help**

Ideally, with help from an IR35 expert, you should provide the draft covering letter and confirmation of arrangements, perhaps exchanging a few drafts with your immediate project manager who actually knows what you do, and then ask them to sign it. Don't ask someone from the human resources or legal department to sign it – they don't know how you work and will probably come up with lots of reasons why they shouldn't sign it anyway.

Although it is not always possible, particularly with contractors such as offshore engineers or IT contractors requiring access to sensitive secure internal systems, where there is a genuine need to work on-site within prescribed hours, try to include an opening paragraph about hours and location; this should include statements along the following lines:

- Start and end times of the day are at the contractor's discretion, allowing for factors such as professional courtesy and access to systems and key client personnel
- Where possible and where work schedules and the practicalities of the project permit, the contractor shall be able to work at their own premises.

Where you must comply with time and location constraints, the covering letter should explain why this is required. For example, health and safety or security requirements might only allow access to a site at specific times.

**Avoiding 'mutuality of obligation'**

To get around the issue of mutuality of obligation, in the covering letter you could include the following: 'I would welcome the opportunity to work on additional projects, but I understand that I am under no obligation to do so, and any I do consider are at my discretion. Any work outside the original contract specifications will require a separate specification, negotiation for the rate or project fee, and a separate contract.'

Each contractor will have individual needs, but the core components of the covering letter should include a preamble covering time and location, a bit on control and substitution, a sentence about mutuality of obligation, and, of course, deal with the part and parcel issue.

## Confirmation of arrangements checklist

To accompany the covering letter, a typical confirmation of arrangements would contain the following:

- The precise nature of the services you provide
- The exact dates of your contract
- Confirmation that a substitute can be supplied, at your expense and your choice
- The financial arrangements, such as daily/hourly rates or a fixed fee
- The location of the contract, including other client sites
- Confirmation you can work from your own office
- The reason that you need to be on site, should that be the case
- Confirmation you can't be asked to do something not in your contract
- The fact that you work according to your own hours
- Your client does not instruct you on how to perform your tasks
- Confirmation that you are not governed by the same rules as permanent employees, except for obvious exceptions, like health and safety
- Confirmation that you supply your own equipment, and if you have to use the client's equipment why, for example reasons of security or health and safety
- Confirmation you are liable for damage or loss through negligence

- Confirmation you have to rectify defective work at your own expense
- Confirmation you can work for other clients during the course of the contract
- Confirmation you do not receive any form of benefits enjoyed by full time employees, not even use of the company canteen
- Confirmation that you do not take work not specified in the contract
- Confirmation that if you do not work, you do not get paid
- Confirmation that you could supply a substitute, for example in the event that you are unable to work due to illness.

Ideally, when submitting the confirmation of arrangements with the covering letter, you should also supply a list of your preferred substitutes, possibly even including brief CVs and inviting the client to inspect these potential replacements.

This is becoming an increasingly important document in proving that a contractor is outside IR35, so it is important to have a copy on record for each and every contract you undertake.

**Use client sign off sheet to confirm working arrangements**

A simple and useful alternative to creating a confirmation of arrangements is to use the free client sign off sheet provided with the test report available via ir35testing.co.uk. As step one of your due diligence process it's always best advised that you test your IR35 status online to gauge your level of risk and inform your next decision. After receiving your results, you have the option to purchase a detailed report highlighting your risk factors and advising on how to stay outside IR35.

This includes a client sign off sheet. This can be used to confirm details of your working arrangement as indicated by your test feedback that are not stipulated in your contract. This sign off sheet can prove to be an important part of your compliance file and can be used to further demonstrate due diligence to HMRC and, if necessary, at a later date a tax tribunal.

# 8.6 Setting and managing client expectations

Many clients will have either very little or no understanding of IR35. The sooner you are able to set and manage your client's expectations, the better. Speak to your main contact with the client, probably your project manager, and explain to them very briefly about the key issues covered so far in this chapter.

Ideally, you should broach the topic of the confirmation of arrangements as soon as you feel comfortable. The covering letter will also help to clarify exactly how the relationship will work, and that you are not just another employee but a highly qualified professional brought in to apply your specialist skills to a particular aspect of a project.

**Don't become a 'tail-end Charlie'**

Whatever you do, don't allow yourself to become a 'tail-end Charlie' and take on tasks outside your contract to please the client, or to ramp up billable hours. If HMRC or a judge determines that a notional contract runs on that basis you will be inside IR35.

Remember some client managers might simply be inexperienced at hiring and managing contractors, or divorced from what they mean by the human resources department. To them you might be just like an employee who will do any work they choose to send your way. Contractors need to set expectations right from the start, and throughout the project, and also keep evidence (emails etc.) that conversations like this have gone on.

This tactic is all about one thing: mitigating the chance that the manager/client says something untrue – sometimes in the mistaken belief they are being helpful to you – if the taxman comes knocking on the door. HMRC has been known to ask questions like, "So, tell me Mr Project Manager, how do you control your contractors?" Your client needs to know right from the start that they don't control you.

Think of your relationship with your client like this: if you ask a builder to build a wall, you tell them where and how high, but you don't tell the builder how to mix the mortar and lay the bricks. Clients should extend the same professional courtesy to you.

**Managing expectations – a step by step guide**

Follow these steps to ensure the client knows exactly how the relationship works:

1. Get the confirmation of arrangements signed
2. Make sure you read through this with the manager so they digest everything in it
3. Make minutes about what happened in the meeting when the letter was signed
4. Send a copy to your project manager – and keep a copy of the email in your contract file
5. If you are asked to do something that is not part of the services you are contracted to do, make it clear verbally that you won't/cannot do that. Then send a further email to your project manager – and keep a record of that email and any responses.

Of course, this is the ideal route that you will take, but don't be surprised if the client is reluctant to sign a confirmation of arrangements letter. Traditionally, many clients have sought to avoid signing documents regarding the employment status of the contractor due to concern that it implies risk to their business. Assuring the client that there is no risk to them and that you are merely building up evidence to help prove your IR35 status should be enough to allay any fears and get the document signed.

## Public sector differences

For public sector clients, on the other hand, there is an element of risk. However, you'll likely find that public sector clients are in fact more inclined to agree to sign a confirmation of arrangements. Public sector clients are responsible for determining the IR35 status of the contractors they hire.

Therefore, should you be working on an outside-IR35 contract in the public sector, it is in the client's best interests to confirm that your working practices are those of a *contract for services* arrangement. Alternatively, if the client declines to sign a confirmation of arrangements, you have three realistic options:

- Take the contract as inside-IR35 but add a 20% premium to your fees to counteract the tax loss
- Turn down the contract altogether
- Suggest they hire you on a fixed-term employment basis, with employment rights.

None of these outcomes are attractive to the client who will be keen to ensure they continue to attract contractors without paying out too much money. With experts predicting that the public sector rules will be subsequently rolled out into the private sector, the process of securing a confirmation of arrangements could be a common occurrence for all contractors and clients.

## 8.7 Reaffirming your IR35 status with essential working practices

Your working practices are a crucial factor that will help determine your IR35 status. If you work and act like an independent professional running a business, the likelihood is that you will be treated like one by your client.

So, as well as ensuring you have in place all the requirements of section 5.12, such as your own business cards, laptop or tablet, home office and so on, it is important to demonstrate that you are in business in your own right. This is because you are and every day you are on the client's site you are 'client facing'.

This means ensuring that your working practices change so that you run your company and carry out your work like a proper business, and that your professional working practices and standards adhere to the content of the contract document.

Avoid becoming 'part and parcel' of the organisation by distinguishing yourself as an independent contractor. And if that means you have to maintain your professional distance from colleagues, wear a smart suit to the office every day when all around you are in casual clothes, then do so – stand out as a professional contractor.

Your working practices will contribute hugely to any construction of a notional contract by HMRC, or a judge. If your working practices fail to adhere to the contract and to your position as an independent, professional contractor, it could be deemed not to be genuine and ignored.

## 8.8 Using substitution as a silver bullet to stay outside IR35

Substitution is widely regarded as an IR35 'silver bullet'. If you use a substitute, this means personal service by a named individual is not required and if personal service is not present then you cannot possibly be an employee. Therefore IR35 cannot apply. There is no debate about this – if you can legitimately substitute then HMRC cannot make IR35 stick.

However, be warned that there is always the risk that the taxman may perceive any contractual substitution clause to be a 'sham', believing it not to be valid when subjected to scrutiny. As a result, you need to have the procedures and necessary paperwork nailed down to prove to HMRC that your substitution is genuine in the instance of an investigation.

The right of substitution all hinges around personal service. If personal service is not required, there cannot possibly be a *contract of service* – or employment contract – meaning the contractor cannot be inside IR35.

## Ensuring substitution becomes a 'silver bullet'

Though simply inserting a right of substitution clause alone is not enough to deflect an HMRC investigation negotiating the clause correctly is critical to the process. However, if a valid substitution clause exists and the client acknowledges this when asked by HMRC, the taxman will find it very hard to argue a case that you are inside IR35.

This can be hard for some clients who themselves are employees to accept, as many will believe that they are hiring another employee in spite of the actual contractual requirement. It may be up to you to explain to them that genuine contractors are business-to-business service providers which means they can send another contractor in to work in their place, contract permitting.

The right of substitution must also be 'unfettered'. This means that the client cannot reserve the right to stop you from sending in a replacement, or indeed have any legal rights to vet and approve the substitute. Allowing the client to have any input over who the substitute is will render the clause invalid.

This can make it doubly difficult to negotiate the clause as the client will be keen to ensure that anyone drafted in has the necessary skills to contribute to the project, whilst they may also perceive that you are trying to shirk your responsibilities by sending in a replacement.

**Allaying client concerns with a termination clause**

One way to ease these concerns is to agree to a termination clause should you provide services that do not meet the standards expected in the schedule. You can also point out that the contract legally states that you must fund the handover and cover any necessary training costs.

Once an unfettered right of substitution has been agreed and actually carried out, you need to ensure the paperwork backs this up and establish a paper trail. For example, your limited company should have a business-to-business *contract for services* with the substitute worker's limited company.

The client also needs to know about the substitution for it to be classed as genuine, otherwise it won't be considered valid. For many roles where you are providing services on site, this will become obvious. However, for more remote assignments, you are advised to inform the client that a substitute is being drafted in and keep a copy of the correspondence. In addition, make sure you retain all correspondence with the substitute themselves. This is key to proving to HMRC that your substitution clause is genuine.

## 8.9 Timing IR35 negotiations and contract renewals

Negotiating with the agency, or client if direct, is the only way to remove risky IR35 clauses from the contract. Most agencies who place high end contractors are used to this process, and so it shouldn't be too much of a laborious procedure. There are certain factors that will influence your negotiation position, including:

- Market conditions
- Whether the contract is new or a renewal
- Whether you have already signed the contract.
- Whether it is a private or public sector placement

**Market conditions**

When the market is booming and specific skills are in high demand, contractors are at a clear advantage. Agencies often struggle to source the necessary expertise during these times and have been known to advertise contracts as being 'IR35 compliant' as a selling point, even though a guaranteed IR35 compliant contract does not exist.

In these instances it is often in the agency's best interests to ensure contracts are more IR35 friendly. So it is not unusual for them to actively engage in changing less friendly contracts of their existing contractors to reduce the risk of them leaving the agency for a compliant contract.

In such circumstances where you have agents pursuing you for roles you are well placed to filter out contracts that are not likely to be IR35-friendly. Occasionally, an agent might tell you they can get you a contract at a higher rate even though it is inside IR35.

Alternatively, if you're renewing a contract that is likely to be inside IR35 in a booming market, the likelihood is you'll easily be able to secure a contract outside of IR35 elsewhere. It is worth approaching both your agent and client and using this as to get the contract changed. But of course, if the contract was caught by IR35 in the first place and there is set to be no material difference upon renewal, it's unlikely that you will suddenly find yourself outside IR35. Tread with caution. The better strategy in this instance is likely to be to move elsewhere.

On the other hand, in a depressed market, there is very little room for manoeuvre on IR35 issues for contractors because their bargaining power is reduced. When there is a surplus of contractors available, agents do not have to succumb to requests to get contracts changed to alleviate IR35 concerns, and so it can be hard to get them to budge.

When you have little bargaining power you would be best advised to avoid discussing IR35 with the agent prior to receiving and reviewing a contract, as doing so would weaken your chances of being considered for the role. Once you have received a contract offer, and the agent has already invested a significant amount of time into securing the deal, you are in a much stronger position and should then try to initiate negotiations.

**Contracts up for renewal**

If you happen to be in an inside-IR35 contract up for renewal in a depressed market you are in a stronger bargaining position. The client wants to avoid the cost and hassle of you leaving whilst the agent wants you to renew to continue bringing their commission in. Raise the topic roughly a month before renewal as it could take some time to arrange.

Trying to renegotiate the wording of your contract at renewal time so that it better matches your working practices and conveys that you are outside IR35 involves a specific process. Having an IR35 specialist involved in this process is well worth the investment.

You can look at this as a five step process:

**Step 1:** Get expert IR35 help to compile a list of the changes that need to be made.

**Step 2:** Speak to the agent and request the changes for the renewal. After they refuse (most likely) ask to speak to the person who deals with the legal aspects of the contracts. Trying to negotiate contractual issues with an agent can prove unproductive, as they just want you to sign again and have other more pressing things to attend to.

**Step 3:** Get your professional adviser to speak to the agency's legal person on your behalf. This is much more effective than trying to do it yourself.

**Step 4:** Speak to your client directly if you are not getting results. Tell them you desperately want to renew the contract, but give the impression that you might be forced to consider your renewal position if they cannot get it sorted out. They might put pressure on the agency to compromise.

**Step 5:** You can also use the same 'I'm not sure I want to renew unless you sort out the contract' tactic with the agent. They don't want to appear bad in front of their client by not treating their contractors well. But be careful with this tactic: you don't want to give them a month to find someone else to replace you!

You could spend a tidy sum in legal fees being given the run-around. So try and establish early whether or not the agency is paying lip service and trying to stall you, in the hope that when renewal time comes you'll just sign the contract again.

At some point it may become clear that you are going to be unsuccessful with the changes. There are a few options:

- Grin and bear it. You tried.
- Threaten to not take (or renew) the contract. This might make things happen. But beware of burning bridges.
- Ask for a rate rise. It's unlikely to cover the whole gap, but you might get something.

If a month before renewal you feel you are getting nowhere and could get a better contract elsewhere, then it might be worth looking for one. Having a back-up plan is always useful.

Bear in mind that getting individual contracts changed for contractors at a site where the agency has many other contractors is hard. They will have their upper level contract with the client and the lower level contract with you. Changing your contract means either opening up a risk to them if they don't change their contract with the client, or spending money changing it.

Also, as most agencies don't have separate legal departments and lawyers are expensive, agents will try and prevent any changes getting made. Understanding this when you approach them, and making it as simple and inexpensive as possible to make the changes you want, will give you a much higher chance of success.

However, as has been highlighted, the case of Autoclenz Ltd v Belcher & Ors [2011] proved that working practices can often override what is written in the contract itself in a tax tribunal decision, providing the evidence is compelling enough. The real relationship between the contractor and client determined by a consideration of the written contracts as well as evidence of working practices is what is known to HMRC and tax tribunal judges as the 'notional contract'.

As a result, whilst it is always advisable to tighten up your contract upon renewal time, if your working practices put you outside IR35, it may not be absolutely necessary as you should have sufficient evidence to mount a strong defence if you are challenged by HMRC. However, this also reinforces the importance of building a compliance file to prove your outside-IR35 status. This is discussed in more detail in section 8.10.

## Negotiating renewals - private and public sector differences

The sector, public or private, your client operates in is another significant factor impacting your chances of successfully renegotiating with agencies, as the IR35 reforms have flipped the dynamic between public sector contractor and agency on its head. Public sector agencies will be far more inclined to help negotiate compliance. This is because securing an outside-IR35 contract for a contractor also makes fiscal sense for them, because they won't be subject to rate rise demands from their contractors.

Remember however, it is absolutely critical that you discuss IR35 prior to signing any contract. Unless market conditions are particularly favourable, it is often a waste of time trying to re-negotiate a contract for IR35 compliance. Agents are always trying to secure new deals to generate more commission, which will often take priority over supporting a previous deal, particularly in the private sector.

## Avoid non-compliant contracts

Even in a booming market you would be advised not to sign a non-compliant contract if offered to you. Instead, stall the agent until a few days before the start date. The agent will probably agree with your request to 'address the issue after signing the contract' but the likelihood is that they are paying lip service.

However, you can use this to state shortly before the contract start date that you will only sign for one month whilst they work to solve the issue of non-compliance as they agreed. You then have a month to make the necessary arrangements and will have the client on side after making a good impression at their organisation.

## 8.10 Building an IR35 compliance file for each contract

Should HMRC start an investigation, then comprehensive, well-organised and accurate business records could make the difference between winning and losing a case.

**In the private sector**

In the private sector your compliance file could prove the difference between a quick and straightforward investigation that HMRC takes no further, and a full investigation that could lead to a negative judgement and a court case.

So, it is essential that you keep a record of each separate contract and schedules for each different project going back six years. It's not a difficult task, and well worth it when you consider the tax savings you're making by staying outside IR35. Remember that HMRC will look for every opportunity to justify its inspection by claiming back-taxes, NICs and penalties, so investigators will want to go through your trading history in detail.

Should HMRC conduct a tax inspection and dispute your status, you will be faced with a tax inspector who will look at your evidence, and then potentially with the First Tier tax tribunal if you appeal. Should you appeal, you are likely to face a tribunal judge. They will all need convincing, with as much proof as possible, of what actually took place between you and the agency, and between you and the client.

## In the public sector

In the public sector, things are not quite so frightening. You should have no liability, as long as you have not deliberately committed fraud. But keeping records is still important, as the evidence you have given to the client may be needed to be substantiated to ensure the onus of responsibility is not passed to you.

## Compliance file essentials

You may have some proof in your letter of engagement. Again this may not be specific enough, but it may help. If you can't get terms into the contract that clearly put you outside IR35, you have to find other means of proof. And even if you have a sound contract, you might need to back it up. So aim to achieve the following:

- Get a signed confirmation of arrangements letter
- Get your project manager to let you do some of the work at home, and see that the email record shows this is taking place. Or simply get a note saying you can work at home
- The right of substitution is a very important proof of being outside IR35. Send the client or the agent emails about this. If you get a reply, that may prove extremely useful. Any other proof of that kind, like letters or notes from the agent or client could help too
- Keep any proof you can get that you've paid your own expenses. Not just receipts, but also any requests for materials needed from the client, any email asking you to pay expenses and so on.

Fill your IR35 compliance file with evidence of your day-to-day working practices – this evidence may seem innocuous at the time, but could tip the balance towards a judge finding you outside IR35. Most aspects of your contract will provide you with an opportunity to add to your compliance file. For each contract, you should attempt to do as much of the following as possible:

1. **Retain correspondence:** Save copies of emails where you and your client discuss key elements of a contract

2. **Maintain a decision diary:** This will describe how you, not your client, made fundamental decisions about how you should do the work on the project, note general issues showing lack of client control, your independence and the application of your special skills

3. **Record important conversations:** Get proof of conversations and events where contractual issues have been discussed, and, whenever possible, get the client to sign the notes

4. **Prove differentiated treatment:** Save emails where a client treats you differently to their employees. For example, the IT systems might go down, and the client may send you an email instructing you to go home when the employees have to stay

5. **Tell, don't ask**: When deciding to take time off, inform the client rather than ask them, and do so via email rather than by using the client's holiday forms or HR system. This demonstrates a degree of control on your part

6. **Get everything in writing:** Should a client express dissatisfaction in your work, get it in writing specifying what needs rectifying before fixing the problem and creating a schedule of the additional work completed to be signed off by the client. You

can't invoice for it but it does demonstrate financial risk on your part

7. **Document tendering for contracts**: This should include time spent on the tender process and expenses incurred, as this also demonstrates financial risk

8. **Document smaller projects:** Document instances where you are asked to deliver a small speculative project or provide free consultancy with a view to winning a much larger contract, including the services delivered, time spent and expenses incurred

9. **Publish your own website:** Keep it up-to-date in order to prove both that you are in business and that the site is being used as a proactive marketing tool

10. **Network with other contractors:** Maintain a database of contractors who can potentially act as substitutes and exchange emails with them to demonstrate to HMRC that you have made each other commitments

11. **Work from home:** Email your client to confirm when working from your home office and record on your invoice the time spent away from the client's site. If the amount of time spent at your home office is over 20%, it's a strong indicator that the client has no control over where you deliver your services

12. **Reaffirm your status**: Ensure you are named as a contractor on any emails sent by your client to their customers to avoid being considered 'part and parcel' by HMRC

13. **Turn down work:** Politely decline to take on any significant tasks that are outside your original remit,

and gather evidence of your refusal to prove you are not controlled by the client.

Make an effort to get as much proof as you can. Remember, HMRC may go back through your contracting history for as many years as it wishes if it decides to investigate you, so you will need to save everything relevant. Make sure that you get proof while the project is taking place, as you'll certainly struggle to obtain it many years later.

# 8.11 Insuring yourself against IR35

An investigation can take years and, if it goes as far as a tax tribunal and appeals, can cost tens of thousands of pounds in defence costs. This doesn't include back taxes, NICs and penalties you might have to pay if you lose; in one case a contractor received a tax bill of £99,000. The financial cost will be considerable; the emotional cost to you and your family could be even greater.

In the UK, if HMRC demands a settlement from you of unpaid taxes, penalties and interest, it is your responsibility to challenge the settlement; if you don't, you will be required to pay up. It is therefore down to you to mount a defence; otherwise you will be assumed to be liable and will have to pay any outstanding taxes, NICs and penalties that HMRC demands.

**Tax investigation insurance**

Contractors subject to tax investigations have few protections. HMRC's investigators can delve into every aspect of your life and use any evidence against you. And because the investigations can take so much time and have such potentially dramatic consequences, it is essential to have professional help to mount your defence.

Fighting inspections and rulings by HMRC is not for the uninitiated. Many cash businesses, even small firms like corner shops, have tax enquiry and investigation insurance that can help considerably with the process. If you choose to take out a similar insurance, do it sooner rather than later so you have maximum cover by investing in a good policy before an inspection starts.

### Tax liability cover

As a contactor in the private sector, as well as investigation insurance, you may be able to take out a tax liability cover policy. In addition to paying the costs associated with running a defence, you would be covered if you lost the case and owed money to HMRC.

The cost of tax investigation insurance is typically in the low hundreds of pounds each year. What makes it a 'no brainer' for most contractors is that if you don't have insurance and need to pay your own costs for a defence, you almost certainly won't get costs awarded, even if you win the case.

In the public sector, it may be the case that the client or agency wishes to be indemnified. If so, there are insurance options available. You could provide this indemnity, or it might be that the client or agency buys the insurance themselves.

## 8.12 Staying outside IR35 if you go contracting for your former employer

Contractors returning to work for a former employer, or being asked to return immediately on a contract basis after redundancy, face a very real threat of being found inside IR35 unless it is very obvious that the working relationship has changed. By continuing to work for your ex-employer immediately after your contract of employment has been terminated, you have no time to establish yourself in the eyes of the taxman as being in business on your own account.

Your client, and former employer, could also be entering a minefield of employment legislation if they hire you, a worker turned contractor who they've just made redundant. Clearly there could be questions put to your employer/client about the legitimacy of their redundancy process.

## Prove your working practices have changed

But it is possible for you to remain outside IR35 when contracting for a former employer; you just have to work that much harder to prove you are not a disguised employee. Not only do you have to avoid falling foul of the standard tests of employment, but you also have to clearly identify and demonstrate how the relationship and working practices have changed since changing status from employee to contractor.

You must actively avoid any old roles that place you in an employee's shoes, like being a fire marshal or first aider. You should sign in every morning, use visitor parking spaces and make sure you are no longer part of company organisational charts and telephone directories, unless clearly identified as a contractor. You should even steer clear of organised staff social events, like Christmas parties, although you can still join your former workmates for an informal drink after work.

## Demonstrate business risk in the contract

If you absolutely have to start on the Monday after leaving on the Friday, then the first contract you work on should ideally be a project with clearly defined outcomes, preferably on a fixed-price basis, rather than an hourly or daily rate. Staged payments on achieving significant project milestones should be written into the contract, leaving little doubt that you, the ex-employee, are now taking a significant business risk.

In addition, you must be confident that not only has your former employer understood the legal and tax implications of the new arrangement, but is also prepared to treat you as a business-to-business supplier. You should also be confident that the former employer would be able to accurately explain and defend the new relationship to an HMRC inspector, and potentially to a tribunal judge.

## 8.13 How to manage bonus payments to avoid IR35

Don't be discouraged from working on a performance-related basis, as that's precisely how many businesses operate. But if you've negotiated a contract where you receive bonus payments, you might find yourself pitched straight into IR35, as HMRC is likely to see such bonuses as being evidence that you are a disguised employee. But you can legitimately receive 'bonuses' and remain outside IR35 if you pay attention to detail.

Something as simple as the wrong word on a document could tip the balance against you in an IR35 review. The first lesson is never to call a bonus a 'bonus', because that is associated with employment.

In fact, that simple word on a contract may be sufficient to spark a full-blown IR35 enquiry. So, if you are offered a bonus during contract negotiations, you should ensure that the contract and surrounding 'paperwork' never refers to the payment as a 'bonus'. The wording should always be amended to say 'incentive' or 'completion' payment.

In addition to correcting the terminology, ensure that the incentive payments are specifically related to a project and will only be paid on completion of milestones, or once the project has been successfully completed and the specifications met.

# 8.14 IR35 issues for project managers

If you choose contracts with project management responsibility, by definition you are there to manage projects, which under certain circumstances could give the impression of disguised employment. But with the right documentation in place, and regular updates made as required, you are likely not to be judged as inside IR35, particularly if it is clear you have no line management responsibility.

Clearly identify the services to be performed, project deliverables and any milestones. This should include creating a confirmation of arrangements, so the client also understands the true situation. Just as importantly, any services that lay outside your responsibility should also be clearly documented, for avoidance of doubt during a later investigation.

If you are directly managing suppliers, signing off work others complete and managing supplier performance, then those project deliverables must be understood by all parties at the outset. Write these deliverables into the contract so they are unlikely to put you inside IR35.

Project management comes with a health warning, because getting involved in any kind of human resources processes with the client is a sure-fire way to subsequently become involved with HMRC in IR35 issues. You should refuse to be involved in their client's formal HR procedures, whether they involve recruitment, performance appraisals or grievance and disciplinary processes.

There may also be employment law implications for the client if they let a contractor implement HR processes, as the contractor may not technically be authorised. Also, by implication, if you do perform those duties you are almost certainly caught by IR35. Line management and project management are not the same thing. If you adopt best practice from the outset, you should emerge from an IR35 investigation unscathed.

# 8.15 IR35 Issues for contractors working overseas

IR35 can follow you across borders when you go contracting overseas. If you remain liable for tax in the UK, then you are liable for an IR35 re-assessment of whether you were actually an employee of a foreign company or whether you were a genuine contractor.

IR35 legislation still applies to you if you're working for a client within any country in the European Economic Area (EEA), as well as for a client in jurisdictions with a 'Reciprocal Agreement' (RA) with the UK regarding tax and social security, including the USA, Canada and Japan.

**IR35 knows no bounds**

Even if you are working for long periods in remote regions, on offshore platforms or on survey vessels, you are still not exempt from IR35 if yourself and your company are UK residents. IR35 knows no bounds, and a series of high profile cases involving tax exiles has led HMRC to tighten the rules regarding tax residency even further.

Your tax residency status usually depends on how many days you spend in the UK during the tax year in question. Fulfilling either of the following two criteria means you are a UK resident for tax purposes:

- You spent 183 or more days in the UK in the tax year
- Your only home was in the UK (you must have owned, rented or lived in this house for at least 91 days in total, and you must have spent at least 30 days there during the tax year.

Fulfilling either of the following criteria means you are automatically a non-resident of the UK:

- You spent fewer than 16 days in the UK during the tax year
- You work abroad full-time (working at least 35 hours a week) and spent fewer than 91 days in the UK (of which no more than 30 were spent working)

When examining you for IR35, HMRC will also look at your ties to the UK, such as your family and your limited company. The more ties it finds, the more likely it is to conclude that you are a UK resident.

**HMRC's statutory residence test**

Rules surrounding tax residency are fairly complicated, and anybody unsure as to their own tax residency should consult HMRC's statutory residence test (SRT), which sets out all of the individual factors affecting tax residency status. However, the large majority of contractors will find that they remain a UK resident.

When you cease to be liable for taxes in the UK, you can forget about IR35, but you will have to think very carefully about the rules in the country you are now working in, because these can be quite restrictive.

HMRC will follow the same procedure that it always does if it wishes to prove that you are caught by IR35. The first step is to obtain a copy of the contract between your end client and the agency you worked for to compare it with the one you have with the agency. If the agency-client contract sounds a lot like an employment contract, you will almost certainly experience the start of an IR35 investigation.

In practice, HMRC may not find it easy to obtain contracts drawn up between two foreign companies, that is, the agency abroad and the end client abroad. HMRC has no jurisdiction outside the UK, and foreign tax authorities are rarely cooperative with each other.

But don't count on avoiding the IR35 issue in this way. Should HMRC manage to obtain what it needs, you could be in trouble. It is best to ensure that your contract clearly addresses the IR35 issues, just as if you remained in the UK.

## Caught by IR35 – do I pay NICs on any deemed payment?

If deemed to be caught by IR35 whilst contracting overseas, it's important to remember that, in theory, you should be making social security contributions to the state in which you are working, so any deemed payment calculation won't include NICs.

Special EEA rules apply if you happen to be working in two member states. In this case, you would be subject to the legislation of the member state in which you reside, which is probably the UK. If you are found to be working inside IR35, the full deemed payment of income tax and NICs will apply. Should the country that you are contracting in have no social security system, again any deemed payment calculation made must include UK income tax and NICs.

## Always adopt IR35 best practice

The best response to this is to always adopt IR35 best practice regardless of where in the world you happen to be working, even if it is more difficult to gather the necessary evidence overseas than it would be in the UK.

This is very important as it is not uncommon for HMRC to contact overseas clients during an investigation if it doesn't consider a contractor's evidence that the contract is outside to be sufficient.

Although the taxman doesn't have the power to compel a client based outside the UK's tax jurisdiction to answer any IR35-related queries, it does have wide ranging international arrangements to help combat tax evasion, including countries which the UK shares a double taxation agreement with.

Requesting that your client snubs the HMRC's advances won't work either, as it will likely delay the closure of the review. From here, you could find yourself being brought before a tax tribunal and found to be inside IR35, even if you are not. Obtaining a signed confirmation of arrangements at the beginning of any overseas contract and maintaining detailed records throughout should close any IR35 review before it gets going.

## 8.16 Trading via an umbrella company

An alternative, albeit far less lucrative, solution to taking the careful measures required to avoid IR35 is to trade via an umbrella company. The PAYE umbrella model is a less favoured trading vehicle than the limited company as revenue is taxed as though the contractor is an employee, meaning take-home pay is significantly lower. However, it remains a popular solution amongst contractors who don't want the trouble of negotiating IR35 or managing their own company.

The 2016 Finance Bill brought with it the confirmation that contractors either caught by IR35 or considered to be under the 'supervision, direction or control' (SDC) of another entity in the contractual chain would no longer be able to claim tax relief on travel and subsistence (T&S) expenses. Unfortunately, contractors who trade via an umbrella company fall within this scope, meaning this relatively minor perk is rarely available.

Umbrella contractors can still offset certain expenses against their tax liability, such as that for computer hardware and temporary accommodation, but the tax savings gained as a result of these expenses won't amount to anywhere near that attained with an outside-IR35 contract. Your best advice is to follow the advice laid out in this chapter to help guarantee yourself the tax treatment that your status as a contractor warrants.

# 8.17 Chapter summary – key lessons for contractors, agencies and clients

## Contractors

- Always conduct your due diligence and don't rush into signing a contract. You have to take responsibility for ensuring compliance.

- An IR35 investigation can go back six years, or up to 20 if HMRC suspects fraud, so maintaining a compliance file for each contract throughout your career is critical.

- Having the client sign a confirmation of arrangements, can greatly aid a successful defence against an IR35 investigation.

## Agencies

- Contractors will often want to negotiate amendments to the contractor-agency contract to eradicate any IR35-unfriendly features.

- Agencies who are not prepared to negotiate may find contractors won't work with them.

- Public sector agencies can help contractors stay outside IR35 which will greatly reduce further administrative costs and retain contractors.

## Clients

- Public sector clients should evaluate the status of their contractors using online solutions and professional contract reviews to reach accurate decisions.

- Contractors may be able to claim certain employment rights from your organisation if they are forced into an inside-IR35 contract.

- Contractors will often ask for certain arrangements or discussions to be confirmed in writing to help prove their outside-IR35 status.

# 9

# IR35 reviews by HMRC

# 9.1 Protecting yourself from an IR35 review

For most contractors, an HMRC IR35 review, also referred to as an investigation or inquiry, can come as a surprise, and you may not consider there to be any reason for you to be investigated. However, with due diligence and preparation, it need not cause too much anxiety, and if you have taken all the steps recommended in this book, it can actually prove a relatively quick and easy process.

The actual impact of an investigation may differ between the public and private sectors, and the public sector reforms have brought about some fundamental differences between how IR35 investigations apply in either sector. Some key points in this chapter will still apply to all contractors, but there are also some issues concerning IR35 investigations in the public sector that HMRC is yet to cast any light on.

For this reason, this chapter signposts each section that applies solely to the private sector, whilst section 9.14 explains what we know so far about the impact of the public sector reforms on public sector IR35 investigations. Any section that isn't signposted will apply to all contractors.

### Complacency costs contractors

If your evidence and defence are already in place because you've used IR35 best practice and taken care over things like your contract and your working arrangements, plus kept a detailed compliance file, there is every chance that the investigators will be satisfied that you have been correctly working outside IR35, and move on to another case.

Unfortunately many contractors and clients do not pay enough attention to IR35 issues upfront and are 'low hanging fruit' to an inspector. As a result, a private sector contractor may have no defence and find themselves asked to pay the settlement figure. If they decide to fight, it could take many months or even over a year to resolve the case, ultimately leading through the tax tribunals and beyond.

A public sector contractor may not be targeted for an IR35 investigation, but is likely to be called on as a witness. It's absolutely essential that contractors cooperate with their clients and agencies and address any IR35 issues at the beginning and throughout the duration of their contract.

Even if you have done absolutely everything as you should, you should still tread very carefully throughout every step of an investigation. Remember, unlike other parts of the UK law, when you are dealing with HMRC you are liable to pay any settlement until you can prove that you shouldn't have to; it is your responsibility to appeal.

The rules of evidence are not as strict as they are in criminal law, so even a light-hearted, off-the-cuff remark can take on huge significance if your case goes to court. So take great care.

It helps to have an understanding of what is going to happen so you can prepare yourself, and potentially help prepare your client or agency if operating in the public sector. Don't confuse an 'IR35 review by HMRC' with a contract review by an IR35 specialist. HMRC calls its status enquiries an 'IR35 review' when investigating a contractor suspected of being inside IR35, and also uses the phrase in its guidance. A contract review is where you pay an IR35 specialist to go through your contract and highlight any elements that are IR35-unfriendly or commercially undesirable.

## 9.2 How HMRC targets contractors for IR35 reviews

HMRC has multiple routes to identify contractors it believes are at 'high risk' of being inside IR35. It can find you via your clients or through analysis of its own and other government agency databases.

An experienced HMRC inspector can glance at the profit and loss account of a large business, like an engineering firm, oil and gas company or bank, and immediately spot unusually high bills in the professional services costs line. That means the firm probably uses a lot of contractors, which will be of immediate interest to the inspector.

HMRC then only has to identify the contractors from their invoices in the firm's accounting records, and for the inspectors it has suddenly become a target rich environment, with contractors firmly in their sights.

### When does the investigation begin? [Private sector only]

The investigation starts when the inspector reviews the contractor's accounts. HMRC has an extremely sophisticated IT set-up that allows it to data mine its own and other government agencies' databases. An inspector can drill down into your accounts and other records held by government agencies. Any anomalies in your tax records such as mistakes and late payments or fluctuating expenses and income will be quickly and easily spotted. It's the equivalent of having a big red flashing light next to your company name saying, 'look at me, look at me!'

Classic contractor behaviours that used to trigger IR35 reviews, such as paying a low salary and high dividend, are unlikely to lead to an investigation. HMRC's specialist IR35 teams, and not local offices, determine who to investigate and why. However, HMRC is on the lookout for opportunities to generate a good yield from its compliance activity, particularly from higher earning contractors, so you should focus on not attracting attention.

## 9.3 How to avoid being targeted for an IR35 review [private sector only]

In the private sector, the best strategy to avoid an investigation and challenge by HMRC is to avoid being noticed in the first place.

### Making mistakes and late filing attract attention

A guaranteed way to get on HMRC's radar is to submit tax paperwork late and/or with errors. An inspector will work on the principle that if you have made mistakes with, for example, your Corporation Tax return, you are probably making other mistakes that could lead to an incorrect tax calculation.

This is easy to fix, and you should take simple steps such as hiring an accountant to file your tax returns and other tax paperwork accurately and on time. In fact, simply having your accountant named on your tax return should be enough to detract attention from HMRC.

You should always do what you can to avoid making a 'generalist' tax inspector think IR35 might apply. Although major HMRC offices such as Cardiff handle things like tax returns, they will refer a contractor's case to a central specialist IR35 team if they believe that IR35 could apply.

### Accounts analysis

Because HMRC uses a range of sophisticated software to analyse all the data available on individual taxpayers, contractors may be at risk of being investigated without even realising it. HMRC has dedicated teams that use data mining and analysis to flag potential targets for investigation. So, if you are particularly profitable one year and much less so the next, HMRC's software will spot this and flag the case for a human tax inspector to review.

You may be able to avoid this type of investigation simply by including explanatory notes on your tax return. HMRC will actually accept a reasonable explanation as to why expenses might be particularly high when compared to previous years, which could halt a potential IR35 investigation.

### IR35 best practice

There is no substitute for good, old-fashioned IR35 best practice. You should begin each contract with a contract dossier that will begin with acquiring their own evaluation using an online IR35 tool, such as ir35testing.co.uk. This will provide the necessary assessment needed to determine whether they should secure an expert contract review. This would be carried out prior to accepting the contract and securing a confirmation of arrangements signed by your client. It will then include all the emails and meeting notes that point to the contractor being outside IR35. Ideally, it will also include an example of a substitution.

You should be able to produce a dossier for each contract. That way, if your contract is investigated by HMRC, the IR35 specialist paid for by your tax investigation insurance has all the ammunition needed to quickly shut down an investigation, or to persuade the taxman not to pursue it.

It takes remarkably little effort for you to adopt IR35 investigation-avoiding strategies. But the effort is well worthwhile if it results in killing an investigation before it gets off the ground.

# 9.4 All IR35 reviews start with a letter from HMRC [private sector only]

All IR35 reviews start with a letter from HMRC. Once, IR35 reviews were dressed up as an employer compliance review about payroll, or perhaps as a request to confirm or clarify a fact on a contractor's tax paperwork. Although this still happens occasionally, the majority of IR35 reviews are instigated by specialist teams within HMRC comprising IR35 experts. These teams tend to be more direct. So, if you receive a letter including something similar to the following, which is a real extract from a typical HMRC IR35 review letter, then you know you have been targeted:

*"Will you please tell me whether you have considered the possibility of the company being subject to what is commonly referred to as the IR35 legislation? If you have, and have concluded that the company is not subject to that legislation then please explain to me the basis upon which you arrived at that conclusion. I am asking this to help me be fully aware of and understand any view you may hold on the application of the IR35 legislation."*

### 'Schedule 36 powers'

Since 2009, HMRC has wide-ranging powers to request evidence using 'Schedule 36 powers'. These powers give the taxman the right to request "information relating to the affairs of a taxpayer past, present and future". So it is possible that the letter about IR35 could also include a request for documentary evidence according to Schedule 36, allowing HMRC to issue notices based on the suspicions of one of its officers. Such requests are also known as 'Schedule 36 information notices', or simply 'information notices'.

Using its Schedule 36 powers, HMRC will usually confirm that its interest is not in Corporation Tax or PAYE and will typically ask for three items. These are:

1. **Documents and spreadsheets** that provide a breakdown of the gross income for a specific accounting period. HMRC usually focuses on a particular financial year, which it requires to be supplied within 30 days

2. **Copies of contracts** that give rise to the income breakdowns requested in item 1. This means HMRC want to see all of the contractor's contracts for the financial year under review, also to be supplied within 30 days

3. **IR35 questions**: If it has not included content like the example above, HMRC will ask an IR35-specific question, which will be a variation on: "Please can you tell us whether you have considered the possibility of your contracts being subject to IR35? If you believe that IR35 has not applied in the year in question, please explain the basis of how you arrived at these conclusions."

The final question is key, but it does potentially allow you to close down an investigation before it gains momentum, if an expertly prepared dossier is promptly despatched in response.

# 9.5 When HMRC signals its intention to investigate [private sector only]

Private sector contractors receiving a letter with the IR35 question above or something similar, and/or a Schedule 36 request, should assume that they are in the early stages of an IR35 review by HMRC. You should not respond immediately, but instead seek expert IR35 assistance right away.

If you have tax investigation insurance, contact your insurer before taking any other action. This is normally a condition of such policies, and failure to do so could invalidate your policy. The insurer will have its own roster of IR35 specialists who will represent you, and it is vital that you cooperate fully.

HMRC may suggest a face-to-face meeting, although it is often couched in such terms that it appears to be a demand that you cannot refuse. However, you do not actually have to deal with HMRC face-to-face. HMRC's own IR35 guidance confirms that it can handle the entire case by correspondence.

## Always seek professional assistance

Don't even think of going it alone. Some experienced contractors are highly IR35-savvy, but this does not equip you with the tactics to handle correspondence, a meeting with an inspector, or to provide you with a full understanding of HMRC's powers and tactics.

Even a chance remark to what sounds like a friendly enquiry from a tax inspector can become the basis of a strong case against you. Just to give a real-life example: a contractor who runs a business that uses a lot of sub-contractors on various projects had their IR35 specialist present. The sub-contractors were not employees. However the first question the inspector asked when the meeting began was, 'So, Mr Smith, how exactly do you control your employees?'

Two key IR35 tests were satisfied in that statement; employment status and control. Had the IR35 specialist not intervened at that point and halted the meeting, the client would have responded to the inspector's question as he was invited to do. The inspector would have written in the notes of the investigation: 'When we arrived, Mr Smith explained to us how he controlled his employees.' And this simple statement would have become a conclusive piece of evidence throughout the case, alongside the HMRC inspectors' account of the meeting, during which they would have used similar questioning.

## The costs of failing to comply

Although you should not respond to an HMRC letter without professional assistance, you should respond promptly.

Information notices require the evidence to be supplied within 30 days. If you have a genuine reason why this would prove difficult, such as working on a major tender, then your IR35 specialist can apply for an extension. HMRC used to agree to deadline extensions on an informal basis, but that is no longer the case. Inspectors now insist on reissuing formal information notices to allow for extensions. If you fail to comply with a formal information notice, you can be fined an initial £300 and £60 per day thereafter

Negotiating any HMRC process has become increasingly difficult for non-experts. That's why in most cases, when a contractor has tried to manage the IR35 review without professional help, the HMRC team has outwitted them. The process has become either unnecessarily extended or, in many cases, the contractor has ended up with a hefty additional tax and National Insurance Contributions (NICs) bill. You have been warned!

## 9.6 Steps you can take to shut down IR35 reviews early [private sector only]

Your IR35 specialist will usually try to halt the IR35 review right at the outset. This is typically done by providing a dossier of key written evidence, such as a confirmation of arrangements and evidence of being 'in-business', which clearly establishes that your current and past contracts are outside IR35. The typical steps you should expect your IR35 specialist to take include:

1. Assembling and reviewing the contracts under investigation by HMRC
2. Extracting the information about actual working practices from you, and possibly your client
3. Creating a dossier providing evidence that the contractor is outside IR35.

The dossier assembled to send to HMRC for contractors should include the documentary evidence that focuses on the requirements of the IR35 legislation. It will detail all of the positive pointers, which is why it is so important for you to adopt IR35 best practice at all times, and at every stage of each contract.

For example, one IT contractor who had been targeted by HMRC for a Pay As You Earn (PAYE) employer's compliance review involved their professional advisers from the outset. As a result, the case never even progressed to a meeting and was handled completely by correspondence. The contractor in question was clearly 'in business' and ticked all the right boxes, which included:

- The contractor limited company had a website
- Some client projects were performed on a fixed-price basis
- The contractor had a dedicated and well equipped home office
- The company had made a substantial investment in computer equipment required to fulfil client projects.

This evidence was presented in a dossier to the HMRC inspector with a recommendation that there was no status case to answer. The inspector agreed, and the review was halted before it even got started. Nowadays, these factors alone won't warrant a strong enough case to pass IR35. However, the lesson remains that, in order to mitigate the impact of a challenge, you need professional advice involved from the outset.

## 9.7 Regulation 80 and section 8 – when you know the review is serious

If, during an IR35 review, HMRC decides that some or all of your contracts are caught by the IR35 legislation, you will receive formal notification and a settlement assessment. This is known as a Regulation 80 and Section 8 income tax and NIC assessment and is HMRC-speak for your tax bill as a result of being found inside IR35.

The bill, which has been as high as £99,000 for some contractors in the past, will include back taxes, NICs, penalties and interest. A tough new penalty regime was introduced in April 2009, and you could receive a penalty that can add as much as 70% of your unpaid tax to the settlement assessment.

**Rights of appeal**

The settlement assessment will be accompanied by information about what rights of appeal you have. In almost all cases, contractors will have the right to appeal against the HMRC ruling by applying to the First Tier Tribunal (Tax) to review their case. Under certain circumstances, especially with complex cases or those testing an important point of law, the case can be referred to the Upper Tribunal (Finance and Tax).

HMRC will issue two settlement assessments for all the years concerned:

- Unpaid Pay As You Earn (PAYE) income tax determined under Regulation 80
- Unpaid NICs determined under Section 8.

This is also the stage at which your professional advisors can try to do a deal and negotiate down the assessment. So, for example, if one of the contracts under assessment was borderline, an HMRC inspector might consider doing a deal if you pay the tax and NICs outstanding on the other assessments without appealing. But don't even think of trying this on your own – professional assistance is essential.

Following the assessment, you have 30 days to appeal and request that the case be heard before the First Tier tax tribunal. But the IR35 review is not on hold during this period or whilst you are waiting for the tribunal, which can be many months in the future. There have been frequent examples of last-minute evidence, perhaps from a client who was overseas during HMRC's information-gathering stage, which has swung the case in the contractor's favour.

## Alternative dispute resolution process

There is also the option of HMRC's alternative dispute resolution (ADR) process for small businesses, which can be very effective. HMRC's ADR process involves having the case reviewed by another experienced HMRC investigator, called a facilitator, who has previously had no dealings with the case and whose role is to objectively assist. It is another HMRC inspector, but the ADR process can highlight cases brought by 'awkward' inspectors and many contractors' experience of them has been positive. ADR is often worth trying, because there is no negative impact on a case but it could find in favour of the contractor.

The added advantage of ADR is that it can provide a fast result, with average turnarounds of 45 days, and even complex cases not taking more than 90 days. So ADR could settle an IR35 case without the need to go to a future tribunal that has already been scheduled.

# 9.8 If HMRC rules against you – the appeal process [private sector only]

If everything you have tried in creating an IR35 defence, avoiding notice by HMRC, defending yourself during the investigation and ADR fails, there is still the appeals process. This allows you to appeal to the First Tier Tribunal (Tax) and the Upper Tribunal (Finance and Tax). The tax tribunals replaced the old General Commissioners and Special Commissioners in April 2009, and a key advantage of the replacement system is that it is totally independent of HMRC.

Assuming you've been represented by an IR35 specialist throughout, your professional advisers should offer you their opinion as to whether you are likely to succeed at appeal and in which tribunal. Should they feel your case has a chance of overturning HMRC's settlement assessment at the tax tribunal, then your next step is to appeal the settlement assessment.

The First Tier tax tribunal will be your first port of call to appeal against HMRC's IR35 decision. Ideally, you should have IR35 tax investigation insurance that will pay for the costs of a professional adviser to assist with the case. However, you can download an application form and complete an appeal yourself without a specialist adviser. But this can be risky and is not recommended.

**What happens at a tax tribunal?**

In preparation for the tribunal hearing, HMRC and your advisors each prepare a 'bundle' of evidence for the tribunal judge. HMRC's representative – typically an inspector specialising in appeals hearing work – and your IR35 specialist make their arguments and summations to the tribunal judge.

Either party can introduce witnesses, such as client representatives who may be a witness for your case or for HMRC. You would typically give evidence as well, and all witnesses can be cross-examined. That means you will probably be questioned by HMRC's representative in the tribunal.

Once the hearings are over, the judge will issue a ruling some months later, based on the evidence submitted at the tribunal. If either side chooses to appeal, the appeal is heard in the Upper Tribunal and the hearing process is repeated, sometimes with additional evidence and witnesses.

## If you fail at First Tier tribunal stage

Should you lose at First Tier tribunal you can appeal to the Upper Tribunal (Finance and Tax). Your IR35 specialist may recommend the Upper Tribunal if a point of law is being tested or challenged. Alternatively, if HMRC has lost in the First Tier, it may also apply to have a case heard in the Upper Tribunal. In both cases, the Upper Tribunal is designed to hear appeals where it is thought that the First Tier was 'wrong in law'. This might be where the correct law may not have been applied, where there was not enough evidence, or where the First Tier tribunal did not give adequate reasons for its ruling.

This tribunal is for serious cases that are highly complex and/or are testing major points of law. The Upper Tribunal is what is known as a Superior Court of Record, so its judiciary are both High Court Judges and specialists in finance and tax. Although the rules don't require the contractor to have expert assistance, this is not a tribunal a contractor should not expect to survive without very good professional assistance and representation.

If you win at any stage and HMRC chooses not to appeal, you will walk away with the regulation 80 and section 8 assessments reduced to zero.

## 9.9 What happens if you lose? [private sector only]

If you lose your appeal as a private sector contractor, your limited company becomes liable for unpaid income tax, NICs, interest and possibly penalties. And at this stage it is far too late to try and cut a deal with HMRC. The final assessment is calculated by HMRC based on the deemed payment (see section 10.3) you would have made during the contracts found to be inside of IR35, less a Corporation Tax deduction for the years in question.

HMRC also has the power to impose a penalty. However, if there was no fraudulent intent on your part then HMRC rarely imposes a penalty. Fortunately the number of IR35 cases that work through the entire process are few and you can do a great deal to prevent an investigation ever taking off by always adopting IR35 best practice for all of your contracts.

## 9.10 The IR35 penalty regime [private sector only]

If you knew your contract was inside IR35 and choose to conceal it, or if you are subsequently found inside IR35 following an HMRC review, you could be facing steep IR35 penalties.

An updated penalty regime was introduced by HMRC in April 2009, doing away with the previous negotiated settlement. Prior to April 2009, your tax adviser could negotiate away much of your tax liability and reduce payments; but the new system introduced the concept that taxpayers must exercise 'reasonable care'.

IR35 penalties will be levied when you under-declare your tax liability by not calculating your deemed payment of additional tax and NICs as a result of being inside IR35. These penalties will be still be payable whether you introduced the inaccuracy by being careless, by deliberately not calculating the deemed payment when you knew were inside IR35, or by deliberately under-declaring and concealing the facts.

The penalty is 30% of unpaid tax if HMRC considers you to have been careless. But the IR35 penalties are really steep if HMRC believes your underpayment to be deliberate: 70% of unpaid tax if you knew they were inside IR35 but deliberately did not make the deemed payment calculation; and 100% of unpaid tax if you knew you were inside IR35, deliberately did not calculate the deemed payment and attempted to conceal the underpayment.

## 9.11 Why IR35 cases can take so long to be resolved

One of the commitments HMRC has made is to reduce the time it takes for an IR35 review to be completed. That's because IR35 cases have historically taken years to resolve: one case, that of engineering contractor Mark Fitzpatrick's company MBF Design Ltd, took seven years to resolve, and at the end the contractor was totally exonerated. Fitzpatrick's experiences of HMRC's IR35 procedures are far from unique and only time will tell as to whether HMRC is genuine about its intention to speed up the process.

There is no single reason why IR35 cases can take so long and there are usually a number of factors adding to the delays. Typically, this is because cases can be complex and depend on expert interpretation of evidence, which takes time to gather. 'Soft' variables, such as the personalities of the HMRC inspector, the contractor and their IR35 specialist, plus the speed and efficiency of the client and agent, who both play a significant role in an IR35 case, can easily add weeks and months to the process.

### Information gathering is time consuming

The first stage in an IR35 investigation is information gathering by the HMRC inspector leading the case. An investigator will want to know the details of each of your contracts for every tax year being investigated. That means that if you are under investigation for several tax years, each with multiple contracts, then a considerable amount of information must be gathered from you, your client and your agency.

If you and your IR35 specialist choose to deal with the process purely by correspondence, rather than through meetings, a simple exchange of letters to answer a basic question of fact can take months.

**Clients can cause delays**

Clients involved in the various contracts being investigated can also add delays. Because the inspector will want to understand the exact nature of the real working relationship between you and your client, the client is typically sent a questionnaire with many questions to answer. This can extend the investigation timeline in a number of ways. If your client responds promptly, the inspector may have further questions based on the client's responses, and even more questions on those responses.

But often your client project manager will pass the inspector's questionnaire to the human resources, or legal or procurement teams in the client's organisation, who may choose not to reply at all, or only to reply in very guarded terms that are unhelpful to both sides. Fortunately, this shouldn't be a problem for public sector contractors, as their clients have an incentive to ensure that any review is closed down as soon as possible, being the party responsible for determining the contractor's status in the first place.

Particularly stubborn or tenacious inspectors, with support from their HMRC managers, have been known to insist on taking cases right through to their conclusion in the courts, even if the evidence is weak, such as in the MBF Design case. Nowadays the scope for 'maverick' inspectors is much reduced, as the tax tribunal system allows taxpayers to request an independent review, albeit from an 'independent' HMRC inspector. But that fresh pair of eyes may well find in favour of the taxpayer.

## 9.12 Using the Taxpayers' Charter during an IR35 review

Contractors can use HMRC's Taxpayers' Charter to help with tax and IR35 investigations when the taxman has stepped over the line. Several of the taxpayers' rights listed in the charter can be used to directly help you when being put under undue pressure by an inspector.

The Taxpayers' Charter is HMRC's own document that describes how it will interact with taxpayers such as contractors. The very first clause in the charter states that HMRC will respect you and that it will be courteous and listen to any concerns. However, the charter can be neglected during tax disputes with HMRC when the taxman forgets that it has an obligation to 'respect you' and 'treat you even-handedly'.

If you believe that your inspector is one of the 'awkward squad', then ensure your IR35 specialist is using the charter alongside all the other tools and strategies available to secure a favourable outcome for your case.

## 9.13 Grounds for suing your agent if you are caught by IR35

So you've been found inside IR35 and want to pass the blame to your agency, claiming you were not told the full story and that the contractual terms implicating you were withheld. Unfortunately, the grounds for taking legal action and seeking financial redress from your agency are few, and you face an uphill struggle from the outset.

Your tax affairs are ultimately your problem, not the agency's or the client's. Unless an agency can be proven to have been dishonest in their dealings with you, then a successful legal challenge is unlikely.

However, if you are contracting in the public sector, all of a sudden the reforms mean your tax affairs are of importance to both the agency and client. Given that the client will be held responsible for determining your IR35 status at the beginning of the contract, and will probably assume liability for back taxes, penalties and interest, this section is unlikely to apply to you.

**The influence of the agency**

Your IR35 status will depend on three factors:

- The reality of the contractor's working relationship with the client, which includes the 'notional contract';
- The actual contractual terms; and
- Other evidence that suggests you are in business on your own account.

You have some control and influence over all three factors. But as for the agency, it only has 'control' over the contract, to the extent that the agency influences its contents. What that means is that you are in the better position to influence two of the major factors on which your IR35 status will be tested. So, when considering whether to accept a particular contract, you must exercise your business judgement – and accept responsibility for the consequences of your decisions.

Taking responsibility means following through to make sure any IR35-friendly terms of the contract are actually stuck to. For example, if a contract shows the client has no 'control' over you, yet you arrive on site only to find that the client tries to boss you about, thereby exercising control and placing you at greater risk of being found to be inside IR35, it is your choice as to whether you should accept this, or challenge the client. There are only two sets of circumstances in which you may have grounds to take legal action against an agency if your contract is found inside IR35 and you suffer financially as a result:

- If in the contract, the agency has made an express assurance which has been broken, or which events have subsequently shown to be untrue, and (in either case) if that has a material adverse effect on your IR35 status
- If the agency misrepresented the contract opportunity to you, you took your decision to enter the contract relying on that misrepresentation, and the result had a material adverse effect on your IR35 status.

You have to prove that the agency was at fault and that the agency misled you. In addition, many agency contracts have exclusion clauses that disallow you from taking action where the misrepresentation is innocent or negligent. It is not however generally possible to exclude liability for fraudulent misrepresentations – one which the person who gave it knew at the time to be false.

## Fraudulent misrepresentation

Where your agent made an untrue statement and they knew it to be untrue when they were making it, this qualifies as fraudulent misrepresentation and, under these circumstances, you may have a case. You would have to show fault on the part of the agent, show that you had actually been misled by the agent and relied on the misrepresentation, and also prove you suffered loss as a direct result of having done so.

There have been no publicised cases where a contractor has been found inside IR35 by HMRC and successfully litigated against an agency. It's an untested area.

If you have any doubt about the contents of a contract under negotiation, you should always seek professional advice – it's a small investment compared to the money that would be lost if HMRC found a contract to be inside IR35.

# 9.14 IR35 reviews in the public sector

The IR35 compliance burden in the public sector may instead rest with the client and agency, but it's still very important for contractors to take the necessary protective measures to ensure their contract isn't subject to an IR35 investigation.

Though not yet confirmed, many experts speculate that the client or agency will be the target for HMRC in the instance of an investigation. However, any review into the working arrangements will still require your involvement as you will likely be called on as a witness. You may not be liable for any backdated tax, penalties or interest, but you will still want to contribute to a strong defence to ensure that your future income from contracting with the client doesn't suffer from a tax increase of up to 20%.

There's also the risk that any review could prompt a look into your historic contracts which, if deemed to be inside IR35, you may well be liable for. Clients and agencies may also ask you to indemnify them against any negative IR35 judgement, in which case a strong defence will be crucial.

**Public sector is no excuse for complacency**

Some contractors might be guilty of resting on their laurels and neglecting their due diligence simply because they assume they may not suffer any tax liability. Don't be one of them. Remember, you still have your outside-IR35 contract to potentially lose, and the risk of being caught within IR35 is arguably now even greater in the public sector.

Public sector clients and agencies, the majority of whom will have little prior experience of IR35, need to be informed of its dangers and the steps they may need to take to mitigate their risk, and part of this responsibility rests on your shoulders.

## What might trigger an IR35 investigation?

With the compliance burden in the public sector falling with the client and agency, the focus of HMRC inspectors also shifts. Rather than identifying candidates for investigation by analysing the tax affairs of contractors, as is the case in the private sector, HMRC will instead first look at the inner goings on at the client's organisation and potentially the contractor's agency.

An experienced HMRC inspector may be able to tell whether a large public sector client uses contractors simply by looking at their profit and loss account. Any client that engages a lot of contractors is likely to be a prime target for an inspector, heightening the need for vigilance from all parties.

Using HMRC resources to evaluate a contract for IR35 could also trigger a review from the taxman. HMRC's contract review service and helpline should be treated with caution, as the taxman may be alerted to the affairs of contractors deemed to be outside IR35 who have shared certain information via these platforms. Contracting in the public sector, you need to make sure you stress the importance of using alternative independent IR35 assessment solutions to your client, such as ir35testing.co.uk.

## Using IR35 best practice to avoid an IR35 review

It is not yet fully understood exactly how HMRC intends to scope out its targets, though the taxman will want to see evidence that the necessary measures have been taken to correctly determine the contractor's status by the client. For this reason there is no better way of avoiding an IR35 review than by applying IR35 best practice.

The client needs to be made aware of the potential of an HMRC investigation, but also of the steps required to avoid one. Being able to produce a contract dossier when approached by HMRC should shut down any investigation before it has even begun. This will involve cooperation between the contractor and client, and will contain various items of evidence to demonstrate due diligence and the fact that the contractor is outside IR35, including:

- Evaluation of IR35 status from an online IR35 testing tool (not HMRC's)
- Evidence that the contractor has acquired a contract review from an IR35 specialist
- A confirmation of arrangements, signed by the client
- A collection of emails and meeting notes, highlighting that the contractor is outside IR35

In the private sector it can prove more difficult to gather this dossier, with clients less likely to cooperate as it doesn't benefit them in any way. Fortunately, the public sector reforms mean your client will be more inclined to help contribute towards a body of evidence, being the party responsible for checking your status in the first place.

**Clients need professional assistance**

Your client may be tempted to try and navigate an IR35 investigation alone. However, it's absolutely vital that you make sure they seek professional assistance. Using the body of evidence gathered through IR35 best practice, an IR35 specialist paid for through tax investigation insurance has everything they need to prove to the taxman that no investigation is necessary. This ensures that there is no risk of liability for the client, and that the remainder of your contract isn't subject to excessive taxation.

This isn't the only benefit of acquiring assistance from an IR35 specialist. Should HMRC decide to proceed with an investigation into your contract, there is nobody better placed than an IR35 specialist to help the client navigate the taxman's tricks.

HMRC inspectors are known to employ certain tactics, such as asking leading questions that invite an answer an inspector can manipulate to the taxman's gain. Having no prior experience of IR35, the client will be more prone to fall victim to this.

As such, you should reinforce the importance of engaging an IR35 specialist who can sit in on any meeting or influence any correspondence to ensure that the client doesn't fall victim to any such tactics.

## When HMRC signals its intention to investigate

It may not be as clear from the outset for public sector contractors if their contract is under review by the taxman. HMRC will likely approach the client first, meaning close correspondence between the contractor and client regarding such matters is essential.

If your client has purchased tax investigation insurance, instruct them to contact their insurance provider before doing anything else. Quite often such policies include the condition that the insurance provider is contacted before any other action is taken, so failure to do so could invalidate the client's policy.

The likelihood then is that you will be called on as a witness. In the same way that a contractor's tax expert will brief the client on what to say in the private sector, the client's tax expert will probably want to instruct you with regards to your witness statement.

HMRC is likely to approach your client and propose a face-to-face meeting. However, the client should be made fully aware that this is by no means compulsory, no matter how much the taxman dresses up its request to make it appear to be a demand. HMRC's own IR35 guidance confirms that it can handle the entire case by correspondence.

## What happens if you lose in the public sector?

With clients and agencies undertaking the IR35 compliance burden, it is generally agreed that one of these two parties is set to assume liability for unpaid tax, penalties and interest should HMRC determine that your contract is caught by IR35.

However, it is also likely that some client and agencies will try to pass their tax risk onto their contractors by way of indemnity clauses in their contracts. This is something you must look out for and try to avoid agreeing to if you are working in the public sector.

The final important point to remember is that you are liable for any unpaid tax, penalties and interest if HMRC finds that you deliberately deceived your client into finding you outside IR35 when determining your status by providing fraudulent evidence.

# 9.15 Chapter summary – key lessons for contractors, agencies and clients

### Contractors

- Make sure your tax records don't include any anomalies, such as fluctuating expenses or late payments. HMRC will see it as an open invitation to investigate you.

- Create a dossier for each contract containing evidence proving your outside-IR35 status. It will prove key to immediately shutting down any investigation.

- When chasing taxes HMRC can also issue you penalties of an extra 30% on top of your tax liability. If your underpayment is deemed deliberate, this can rise to 70%.

### Agencies

- Should a contractor that you engage be subject to an HMRC IR35 investigation, the taxman may chase your agency up looking to gather information from you regarding any contract you have held with the contractor.

- If an assurance is made or an opportunity is presented to a contractor within the contractor-agency contract that is subsequently found to be untrue and has an adverse effect on their IR35 status, they have grounds to sue.

- Prior to signing a contract, a contractor will typically get a contract review to identify any IR35-unfriendly

features and try to negotiate them out to avoid an
IR35 investigation.

## Clients

- If you are a public sector client, you are responsible
  for determining your contractor's IR35 status and so
  HMRC may target you for IR35 reviews. Close
  cooperation with each contractor is required to
  ensure you're well prepared.

- Upon agreeing a contract, you can expect the
  contractor's IR35 specialist to contact you requesting
  information about actual working practices. This is to
  help form a body of evidence should HMRC conduct
  an IR35 investigation.

- During an investigation, HMRC may ask leading
  questions, such as: 'How do you control your
  employees?' Beware of this, as responding as you
  are invited to do so could form a conclusive piece of
  evidence against the contractor.

# 10

# Contractors caught by IR35

# 10.1 What happens if you are caught by IR35?

If, despite all the strategies you have adopted and expert advice you have taken, the nature of your assignment means you consider your contract to be inside IR35, then don't panic. The worst that can happen is that you will pay some extra tax for the duration of your current contract. That's painful, but does not mean the end of your contracting career. You can learn from this experience and ensure your next contract is outside IR35.

The intermediaries legislation includes measures you should adopt if you are caught by IR35. Remember that IR35 is there to ensure people who are working like employees pay tax like employees, so what you do next is work out how much extra tax you should be paying, and budget accordingly.

**Private sector contractors**

If you're a private sector contractor, IR35 allows you to set aside some expenses, and then applies income tax and National Insurance Contributions (NICs) to the rest of your income. This is the 5% rule and deemed payment. However, with experience of implementing IR35 spanning as far back as 2000, most contractor accountants will advise you to pay yourself all earnings via a salary using Pay As You Earn (PAYE), which achieves the same ends as the complicated route of calculating and processing the deemed payment.

**Public sector contractors**

If you're contracting in the public sector and contracting via an agency, the agency will assume responsibility for operating PAYE and calculating, reporting and paying tax and NICs via real time information (RTI). If you are contracting direct with a public sector client, they will assume this burden. In both cases your tax is deducted at source prior to you receiving payment.

However, experts have warned that public sector agencies and clients will rarely have all of the necessary information to make the correct calculation, which involves accounting for all allowable deductions including pension contributions, expenses and capital allowances. As a result, your accountant will be working overtime to correct each calculation and ensure that you pay the right amount of tax.

Alternatively, you may prefer not to operate the complicated RTI via your limited company and instead trade via a PAYE umbrella company for this particular contract. Don't be surprised if the agency prefers that you do this too, as many simply won't have the processes in place to manage RTI.

## 10.2 Treatment of expenses and the 5% rule

### Private sector contractors

If you receive income caught by the rules of IR35, HMRC asks that you carry out a deemed salary calculation each tax year, based on income received from relevant engagements. It's worth checking with your accountant about this calculation, but the basics follow.

HMRC allows an expense allowance equal to 5% of the income received from relevant engagements in calculating the deemed salary. This is intended to cover the following 'administration' costs:

1. Premises costs, including home as office
2. Administration and secretarial support
3. Accountancy and tax advice
4. Costs of seeking contracts
5. Printing, postage and stationery
6. Employer's and Public Liability Insurance
7. Training costs

8. Computer equipment (if not eligible for capital allowances)
9. Bank and overdraft interest
10. Hire purchase payments

The 5% deduction is given at a flat rate on gross fees receivable and is not available to employees as an expense which they can draw from the company. It is simply allowed in the deemed calculation of IR35 salary as a fixed and limited claim against the above expenses. In granting the 5% allowance, HMRC does not require proof of expenditure and the full 5% is granted, even if there is no actual expenditure whatsoever.

The 5% allowance is only for 'administration' and is to cover the ten points above. In addition to the 5% for administration costs, a contractor can also claim direct costs such as travel, IT hardware costs, direct training, sub-contractors and so on. Legitimate business expenses not covered by the ten points can be claimed on top.

## Public sector contractors

HMRC has decided to remove the 5% allowance for notional expenses for public sector contractors, claiming its withdrawal makes it easier and less burdensome for agencies and clients to calculate tax deductions. The taxman also claims its decision reflects the fact that contractors no longer have the administrative burden of deciding whether or not the rules apply.

However, HMRC's draft legislation does instruct that the agency or client deducts expenses when calculating tax on the payment to the contractor's limited company that would have been deductible from the taxable earnings if two conditions are met. These are:

a) That the worker had been employed by the client

b) That the expenses had been met by the worker out of those earnings.

# 10.3 How your taxes are calculated

**Private sector contractors**

There are some odd terms used, like 'Net Result' and 'Deemed Payment', but actually, the concept is very simple. Basically, the way it works is you run your company as normal, paying yourself a salary, and claiming the expenses that you are allowed before seeing what is left in the pot at the end of the year.

This then has to be considered as paid as salary from an employer. So a calculation is done to work out what the salary would be ("deemed payment"), a figure which employer's National Insurance Contributions (NICs) would then be applied to.

E.g. Net Result = Deemed Payment + Employer's NICs

Then the employee's NI and PAYE is applied to the deemed payment, just as taxes are applied to salaries.

In practice, most contractors caught by IR35 take everything they earn as a salary along the way, so there is only a small deemed payment, if any, at the end of the year. In fact, most accountants would recommend simply treating all contracting income as salary once you find you are inside IR35, as it is more straightforward than calculating a deemed payment.

However, if you choose to go down the deemed payment route, your accountant will be able to help, and you really don't have to worry about it yourself. But here's a typical example:

Contractor details:

£80,000 annual revenue, £9,000 salary, and £5,000 legitimate expenses.

| | |
|---|---|
| Revenue | £80,000 |
| Allowable expenses (5% of revenue) | £4,000 |
| Salary | £9,000 |
| Legitimate expenses | £5,000 |
| Net result | £61,770 |
| Additional Employer's NI due | £7,490 |
| Deemed payment | £54,280 |
| Additional Employee's NI | £4,485 |
| Additional PAYE | £14,512 |

## Public sector contractors

For public sector contractors, the calculation of taxes is far trickier. Your agency – or in cases where an agency isn't present, your client – is responsible for deducting your taxes and NICs at source via PAYE, as well as paying employer's NI. HMRC insists that tax is reported through the real time information (RTI) process.

This may make it appear relatively simple from a contractor's perspective. However, your agency or client almost certainly won't have sufficient information to make the correct calculation. HMRC's instructions assume that the agency or client is able to identify all allowable deductions such as pension contributions, expenses and capital allowances. This simply isn't the case.

Unfortunately this means that there is a good chance that your tax calculation, as determined by the agency or client, will be incorrect. Subsequently your accountant will have a significantly increased workload as they seek to correct your tax calculation both for your accounts and your self-assessment tax return.

The 5% allowance for notional expenses has been removed, although HMRC's draft legislation indicates that providing proof of allowable business expenses alongside each invoice sent to the agency or client may help to reduce your tax liabilityIt remains to be seen how this will play out in practice.

## 10.4 When you have a mix of contracts – some caught, some not

During your accounting year you may earn revenue from several contracts. Some of which will fall inside the scope of IR35 and others outside. Some may be in the private sector and others in the public sector. These are all factors that need to be accounted for in your accounting records.

### Contracts outside IR35

If you're working an outside-IR35 contract, the tax treatment of your contract and the necessary procedures you undertake will be the same regardless of whether you're in the private or public sector. You'll operate the same way that you would have prior to the public sector changes, trading just like any other limited company business.

Corporation Tax is calculated once your business expenses, including any salary you might pay yourself, have been deducted from your turnover. This is paid on an annual basis based on your 'Corporation Tax accounting period', which is usually the same as your company's financial year.

Dividend payments made out of your limited company throughout the year must be declared and tax is paid on payments received at two intervals throughout the year via self-assessment.

Income tax and NICs are then payable on the salary that you pay yourself out of your limited company. However, you'll find that most contractors pay themselves a low salary below the NICs threshold, receiving the remainder of their income via dividends, in order to increase tax efficiency.

Managing the finances of your limited company is obviously an involved process, which is why the majority of contractors hire accountants. To understand how to set up and run a contractor limited company, see the guide material available at ContractorCalculator.co.uk.

**Contracts inside IR35 – private sector only**

For private sector contracts caught by IR35, receipts and payments for those contracts will need to be identifiable for use in a year-end calculation and your accountant will have to do a different set of calculations for each contract. At the end of each tax year calculations for 'deemed salary' for each contract will be needed to take into account the contract income and expenditure relating to those specific contracts that are caught inside IR35.

Any salary you pay yourself during the year can be allocated to your inside-IR35 income, so that any company profits, excluding salary payments generated by the outside-IR35 income, can be either paid out as dividends to shareholders or left in the company as shareholders' funds for distribution in a future year.

**Contracts caught by IR35 – public sector**

The public sector IR35 reforms mean that your public sector client has the responsibility of determining your IR35 status. The entity closest to you in the supply chain whom you invoice and get paid by is called the "Fee Payer", which is often an agency. The Fee Payer is responsible for calculating, reporting and paying your tax at source.

Your agency may be keen for you to trade under a PAYE umbrella company for these contracts, however, as it means they will not have to undertake the complicated RTI process that HMRC insists upon.

If you do work an inside-IR35 contract directly through an agency, you will have to provide certain information for them to deduct the necessary tax and NICs, including:

- Your name
- Your address
- Your National Insurance number

## 10.5 Can contractors caught by IR35 claim employment rights?

If you have been caught by IR35 and are being taxed as if you were an employee, you may be tempted to go for the 'nuclear option' and try to claim employment rights from your client using the Employment Appeals Tribunal (EAT). Many contractors see this as a possible way forward if they have been mistreated by the client and/or their contract has been terminated early. However, any decision whether or not to go down this route needs to be fully considered, as there is uncertainty as to how it would pan out in practice.

Here are some of the relevant court cases.

### O'Murphy v Hewlett Packard

The 2001 Employment Appeals Tribunal ruling in the case of O'Murphy v Hewlett Packard created case law effectively barring nearly all contractors from claiming employment rights, even when caught by IR35. The precedent set by O'Murphy v Hewlett Packard requires that for any claim for employment rights to succeed, you will have to prove:

a) That there is a contract between you and your client, and

b) Having first established that there is such a contract, to go on to prove that the true nature of that contract is one of employment.

The essential elements of forming a contract under the UK's legal code must be present. These are that you and your client must have agreed:

a) All the material terms of the contract
b) The 'consideration' (which is usually your payment), and
c) That you and your client share the mutual intent to be legally bound.

## Cable & Wireless v Muscat

However, precedents set in the Court of Appeal case of Cable & Wireless v Muscat [2006] suggest otherwise. Here it was determined that contractor Mr Muscat was an employee of his client Cable & Wireless and therefore eligible for employment rights.

This was in spite of the fact that there was no written contract between Mr Muscat and his client. The judge determined that Mr Muscat, whose contract with the agency Abraxas was a contract for services, was engaged in an implied unwritten employment contract with the client, proving that employment rights can be claimed in specific circumstances.

## Using EAT to avoid being forced inside IR35

Historically, whilst there is anecdotal evidence that indicates that long term contractors with the same client have had success claiming rights from their clients, these successes have normally been achieved via settlements with the client who has preferred to avoid court. Those settlements have also tended to be for redundancy payments.

In the courts, however, the story is different. The courts have generally not supported contractors claiming employment rights and have concluded in a few cases that the contractor making the claim is not an employee.

Bear in mind that "not an employee" is what needs to be proved to stay outside IR35.

The identical set of employment case law is used in both the Employment Appeals Tribunals (EAT) and the Tax Tribunals. So, theoretically both courts could disagree, and it is therefore logically possible to be considered an employee for tax purposes by the Tax Tribunal whilst not being considered an employee by the EAT. Since the inception of IR35 in April 2000 this situation has never arisen.

Contractors who are currently operating outside IR35 and are either told by their client they are now inside IR35, or are investigated by HMRC for IR35 non-compliance can consider these two possible options should they wish to fight the action:

1. Spend lots of time and money trying to fight the client or HMRC by gathering evidence to **prove that you are not an employee** and that you have a genuine contract for services. This would be the 'normal' IR35 defence strategy.

2. Immediately lodge an appeal at tribunal claiming employment rights from the client, and spend time trying to **prove that you are an employee**. The client will be fighting you hard trying to prove that in fact you are not an employee.

The second option sounds perverse, right? But it might just be a win-win strategy for you as a contractor. If you win the case and prove that you are an employee, the pay-out from the client might be considerable. And if you lose the case you have a court decision saying that you are clearly not an employee, which you can use as evidence to prove to HMRC that you cannot possibly be caught by IR35. It seems unimaginable that HMRC would try and prove in court that the original court decision was wrong and overturn your ruling. They have other easier targets to focus on.

Option two will of course result in you burning bridges with your client. But if it was the client that tried to force you inside IR35, resulting in you paying considerably more taxes, then it might be a bridge that you don't mind burning.

## Using AWR to avoid being forced inside IR35

A claim for rights under the Agency Workers Regulations (AWR) may also prove a more fruitful alternative. Experts have pointed out that an AWR claim, which would grant contractor's equal rights to their employee equivalents after a qualifying period of 12 weeks, could be a useful bargaining tool used to persuade the client not to force them into an inside-IR35 position.

Explaining to your client the potential negative consequences of them pushing you into a caught-by-IR35 position might just make them work much closer with you to ensure that the working relationship you have with them is a cast-iron contract for services and not caught by IR35.

# 10.6 Chapter summary – key lessons for contractors, agencies and clients

## Contractors

- When caught by IR35 in the private sector, you are expected to carry out what's known as the 'deemed payment' at the end of the tax year, though your accountant may advise that you simply take your earnings as salary throughout the year.

- If your public sector contract is caught by IR35, it is up to the agency in most cases to deduct your tax. However, any calculation will probably require correcting by your accountant, as the agency won't know the details of all your allowable deductions.

- If your existing public sector client tries to naively force you inside IR35 then explaining the consequences of their decision with respect to employment rights you could now claim might make them reconsider their position.

## Agencies

- If you're an agency engaging a public sector contractor caught by IR35, you may be advised to encourage them to trade under a PAYE umbrella company, or else you will have to undertake the complicated RTI process HMRC insists upon.

- If your public sector clients assess existing contractors as inside IR35 you can expect a lengthy fight with the contractor, which may involve them claiming employment rights under AWR or taking them to an EAT to prove their status.

- For contractors that agree to the outside IR35 position and want to use RTI you will need to acquire certain details from them to be able to process the payments.

**Clients**

- If you're a public sector client, it's your responsibility to determine the contractor's IR35 status. If you consider the contractor to be caught, you need to inform the agency to deduct the necessary tax, or deduct it yourself if an agency isn't present.

- If a contractor is bundled into an inside-IR35 contract, they may attempt to claim certain employment rights from you. Judging from precedents set in previous court cases, they could win even if you don't have a direct written contract with them.

- If you're a public sector client hiring an inside-IR35 contractor directly, it's also your responsibility to calculate and deduct their tax and NICs.

# 11

# The financial impact of IR35 – sample calculations

11. The financial impact of IR35 – sample

# 11.1 The impact of IR35 on net income

The impact of IR35 on the take-home pay of limited company contractors is dramatic. If your current earnings after expenses are over £30,000 per year, and you extract your income from your company using the tax efficient option of low salary/high dividends combination, you will lose between 15% to 20% of your take home pay (income after taxes) if your contract is caught by IR35.

The dividend tax changes introduced in April 2016 have narrowed the gap between the net income claimed by contractors outside IR35 and those caught by IR35, but the tax hit is still considerable.

Table 11.1 shows the harsh realities of how your income will suffer if caught by IR35, with the personal allowance and dividend tax taken into account. It is not pretty, which is why investing in staying outside IR35 by using tools such as ir35testing.co.uk and professional contract reviews, alongside insurance, really does pay for itself.

| Salary | Earnings | Net Income (Outside IR35) | Net Income (Caught by IR35) | Net Income Difference | Net Income Change % |
|--------|----------|---------------------------|------------------------------|------------------------|----------------------|
| £8,000 | £20,000 | £15,200 | £13,387.52 | £1,812.48 | -11.92 |
| £8,000 | £25,000 | £18,960 | £16,225.83 | £2,734.17 | -14.42 |
| £8,000 | £30,000 | £22,660 | £19,064.14 | £3,595.86 | -15.87 |
| £8,000 | £35,000 | £26,360 | £21,902.45 | £4,457.55 | -16.91 |
| £8,000 | £40,000 | £30,060 | £24,740.77 | £5,319.23 | -17.7 |
| £8,000 | £45,000 | £33,760 | £27,579.08 | £6,180.92 | -18.31 |
| £8,000 | £50,000 | £37,460 | £30,417.39 | £7,042.61 | -18.8 |
| £8,000 | £55,000 | £41,110 | £33,130.53 | £7,979.47 | -19.41 |
| £8,000 | £60,000 | £43,810 | £35,551.44 | £8,258.56 | -18.85 |
| £8,000 | £65,000 | £46,510 | £37,972.35 | £8,537.65 | -18.36 |
| £8,000 | £70,000 | £49,210 | £40,393.27 | £8,816.73 | -17.92 |
| £8,000 | £75,000 | £51,910 | £42,814.18 | £9,095.82 | -17.52 |
| £8,000 | £80,000 | £54,610 | £45,235.10 | £9,374.90 | -17.17 |

| | | | | | |
|---|---|---|---|---|---|
| £8,000 | £85,000 | £57,310 | £47,656.01 | £9,653.99 | -16.85 |
| £8,000 | £90,000 | £60,010 | £50,076.92 | £9,933.08 | -16.55 |
| £8,000 | £95,000 | £62,710 | £52,497.84 | £10,212.16 | -16.28 |
| £8,000 | £100,000 | £65,410 | £54,918.75 | £10,491.25 | -16.04 |
| £8,000 | £110,000 | £70,810 | £59,760.58 | £11,049.42 | -15.6 |
| £8,000 | £120,000 | £76,210 | £64,602.41 | £11,607.59 | -15.23 |
| £8,000 | £130,000 | £81,090 | £68,072.23 | £13,017.77 | -16.05 |
| £8,000 | £140,000 | £84,865 | £71,242.06 | £13,622.94 | -16.05 |
| £8,000 | £150,000 | £88,465 | £74,727.89 | £13,737.11 | -15.53 |
| £8,000 | £160,000 | £93,235 | £79,569.72 | £13,665.28 | -14.66 |
| £8,000 | £170,000 | £98,635 | £84,411.55 | £14,223.45 | -14.42 |
| £8,000 | £180,000 | £104,035 | £89,253.37 | £14,781.63 | -14.21 |
| £8,000 | £190,000 | £109,368 | £93,747.92 | £15,619.88 | -14.28 |
| £8,000 | £200,000 | £114,320 | £98,172.35 | £16,147.45 | -14.12 |
| £8,000 | £210,000 | £119,272 | £102,596.78 | £16,675.02 | -13.98 |
| £8,000 | £220,000 | £124,224 | £107,021.21 | £17,202.59 | -13.85 |
| £8,000 | £230,000 | £129,176 | £111,445.64 | £17,730.16 | -13.73 |
| £8,000 | £240,000 | £134,128 | £115,870.07 | £18,257.73 | -13.61 |
| £8,000 | £250,000 | £139,080 | £120,294.50 | £18,785.30 | -13.51 |

Table 11.1 Your fall in net income if your contract is caught by IR35

# 11.2 What rate do I need to achieve my desired monthly income?

With this book, you have everything you need to successfully negotiate IR35 and secure contracts outside IR35. However, if your agency or client insists that you will only be hired in an inside-IR35 basis, you will need to know what rate you need to ask for to maintain the level of take-home pay that you would have received outside IR35.

With the public sector IR35 reforms from April 2017, experts believe that with the shift of the tax liabilities for public sector contractors moving to the client or agency, many will consider adopting a risk-averse approach and try to avoid issuing outside-IR35 contracts.

If you have a contract that began or begins prior to the implementation of the reforms but spans into and beyond April 2017, you'll need to conduct your due diligence to ensure your take-home pay doesn't suffer.

Table 11.2 below shows the increase in your day rate necessary to retain your target monthly net income should you ever need to accept a contract within IR35.

| Monthly net income after tax (Outside IR35) | Daily rate required outside IR35 | Daily rate required inside IR35 | Difference | Difference% |
|---|---|---|---|---|
| £2,000 | £144.76 | £178.84 | £34.08 | 23.54 |
| £2,200 | £159.38 | £196.88 | £37.50 | 23.53 |
| £2,400 | £179.10 | £225.15 | £46.05 | 25.71 |
| £2,600 | £194.14 | £244.06 | £49.92 | 25.71 |
| £2,800 | £209.18 | £262.97 | £53.79 | 25.71 |
| £3,000 | £224.22 | £281.88 | £57.66 | 25.72 |
| £3,200 | £239.26 | £300.78 | £61.52 | 25.71 |
| £3,400 | £260.16 | £332.42 | £72.26 | 27.78 |
| £3,600 | £275.62 | £352.19 | £76.57 | 27.78 |
| £3,800 | £291.10 | £388.12 | £97.02 | 33.33 |
| £4,000 | £323.59 | £408.75 | £85.16 | 26.32 |
| £4,200 | £339.93 | £429.38 | £89.45 | 26.31 |
| £4,400 | £356.25 | £450.00 | £93.75 | 26.32 |
| £4,600 | £372.57 | £470.62 | £98.05 | 26.32 |
| £4,800 | £409.38 | £491.25 | £81.87 | 20.00 |
| £5,000 | £426.56 | £511.88 | £85.32 | 20.00 |
| £5,500 | £468.75 | £562.50 | £93.75 | 20.00 |
| £6,000 | £510.94 | £664.22 | £153.28 | 30.00 |
| £6,500 | £582.42 | £721.09 | £138.67 | 23.81 |
| £7,000 | £656.56 | £775.94 | £119.38 | 18.18 |
| £7,500 | £702.97 | £830.78 | £127.81 | 18.18 |

| | | | | |
|---|---|---|---|---|
| £8,000 | £783.44 | £919.68 | £136.24 | 17.39 |
| £8,500 | £833.75 | £978.75 | £145.00 | 17.39 |
| £9,000 | £882.26 | £1,035.70 | £153.44 | 17.39 |
| £9,500 | £930.78 | £1,092.65 | £161.87 | 17.39 |
| £10,000 | £979.30 | £1,192.19 | £212.89 | 21.74 |
| £10,500 | £1,029.62 | £1,253.44 | £223.82 | 21.74 |
| £11,000 | £1,125.00 | £1,312.50 | £187.50 | 16.67 |
| £11,500 | £1,175.62 | £1,371.56 | £195.94 | 16.67 |
| £12,000 | £1,228.12 | £1,432.81 | £204.69 | 16.67 |
| £12,500 | £1,278.75 | £1,491.88 | £213.13 | 16.67 |
| £13,000 | £1,329.38 | £1,550.94 | £221.56 | 16.67 |
| £13,500 | £1,380.00 | £1,610.00 | £230.00 | 16.67 |
| £14,000 | £1,432.50 | £1,671.25 | £238.75 | 16.67 |
| £14,500 | £1,483.12 | £1,730.31 | £247.19 | 16.67 |
| £15,000 | £1,533.75 | £1,789.38 | £255.63 | 16.67 |
| £15,500 | £1,584.38 | £1,848.44 | £264.06 | 16.67 |
| £16,000 | £1,636.88 | £1,909.69 | £272.81 | 16.67 |
| £16,500 | £1,687.50 | £1,968.75 | £281.25 | 16.67 |
| £17,000 | £1,738.12 | £2,027.81 | £289.69 | 16.67 |
| £17,500 | £1,790.62 | £2,089.06 | £298.44 | 16.67 |
| £18,000 | £1,917.96 | £2,148.12 | £230.16 | 12.00 |
| £18,500 | £1,970.71 | £2,207.19 | £236.48 | 12.00 |
| £19,000 | £2,023.44 | £2,266.25 | £242.81 | 12.00 |
| £19,500 | £2,078.12 | £2,327.50 | £249.38 | 12.00 |
| £20,000 | £2,130.86 | £2,386.56 | £255.70 | 12.00 |

Table 11.2 Your target monthly income if inside IR35

# 12

# The history of IR35

# 12.1 The history of IR35 – an overview

IR35 has attracted controversy since it was introduced in 2000, being criticised by tax experts as poorly thought through by legislators and badly enforced by HMRC. Many organisations since in both the commercial and public sectors, including The Office of Tax Simplification (OTS), the IR35 Forum and the House of Lords Select Committee on Personal Service Companies, have reinforced this criticism.

Over the past few years there have been numerous test cases contributing to case law, a public sector witch-hunt targeting contractors and the announcement of the public sector's off-payroll rules. The BBC has even played a role by introducing a flawed employment test for its on and off air contracting and freelance personnel.

Despite many calls for the abolition of IR35, HMRC continues to champion it and the underlying legislation remains unchanged since 2000.

The new changes from April 2017 are the Public Sector reforms. These shift responsibility for determining IR35 status from contractors to engagers, the most significant event in the history of IR35 since its creation. With experts predicting that the rules will be extended into the private sector, the climate for UK contractors will be even more challenging.

The timeline below details all the highs and lows of IR35 since its introduction to show how we have got to where we are now.

# 12.2 The history of IR35 - timeline

### April 2000: IR35 becomes law

Then Chancellor Gordon Brown announces the introduction of the intermediaries legislation in the pre-Budget speech of 1999. IR35 is later adopted as part of the Finance Act for April 2000.

## October 2002: Lime IT vs Justin

Ms Lisa Fernley becomes the first taxpayer to win an IR35 case at the Special Commissioners.

## March 2003: Synaptek vs Young

IT contractor Gordon Stuchbury loses IR35 case at High Court after judge lists eight factors pointing to a contract for services and five pointing towards a contract of service.

## January 2008: Dragonfly Consulting Ltd vs HMRC

John Bessell, contractor and managing director of Dragonfly Consulting loses £99,000 in an IR35 ruling before the Special Commissioners after being deemed 'part and parcel' of the end-client's organisation.

## January 2008: Datagate Services Ltd vs HMRC

IT contracting company Datagate Services wins significant case before the Special Commissioners, proving that HMRC status decisions can be overturned.

## September 2008: Dragonfly Consulting loses appeal

John Bessell loses appeal against IR35 decision in landmark ruling for contract sector.

### March 2010: Tories promise IR35 review

IPSE (then PCG) secures commitment from Conservative Party to review IR35.

### July 2010: OTS announces IR35 review

The newly formed Office of Tax Simplification (OTS) announces a review of IR35 will be carried out in time for the 2011 Budget.

### August 2010: IR35 status test launched

ContractorCalculator launches its free online IR35 status test, later to become IR35 Testing.

### January 2011: ContractorCalculator Whitepaper

ContractorCalculator publishes its IR35 Solutions Whitepaper in support of the OTS IR35 review.

### March 2011: OTS review of IR35

OTS publishes landmark report recommending IR35 suspension along with an integration of income tax and NICs, or better enforcement.

Chancellor opts for 'better enforcement' of IR35 in 2011 Budget.

### May 2011: IR35 Forum

The IR35 Forum, comprising both HMRC and non-HMRC members, is formed and holds inaugural meeting.

## October 2011: AWR come into force

Government introduces the Agency Workers Regulations (AWR), designed to give temporary workers the same rights and pay as employees.

Limited company contractors are excluded from the rules, allaying fears that the AWR would price contractors out of the market.

## December 2011: JLJ Services vs HMRC

IT contractor John Spencer's company JLJ Services wins partial IR35 victory against HMRC in first ever 'split case' ruling.

Tribunal Judge rules that only the last four of the contractor's seven year contract with Allianz are inside IR35, significantly reducing Spencer's original £140,000 tax bill.

## February 2012: Ed Lester scandal

Then Student Loans Company chief executive Ed Lester exposed by media for being a limited company interim management contractor, prompting a Treasury review into Government use of 'off-payroll workers'.

## May 2012: Business Entity Tests

HMRC introduces framework to better administer IR35, including Business Entity Tests (BETs), compliance teams, helpline and review service.

## July 2012: Autoclenz vs Belcher & Ors

Landmark ruling says working arrangements can override written contracts as team of car valeters with contracts containing substitution clauses are determined to be employees by Supreme Court Judge.

## September 2012: Off-payroll rules

'Off-payroll rules' are introduced. Any public sector client hiring an off-payroll worker for more than six months or earning over £219 a day must ensure the worker's tax affairs are in order.

If the worker cannot prove this, they must either be placed on the client's payroll, operate inside IR35 or resign the contract.

Hundreds of contractors are subsequently subject to unnecessary IR35 reviews as a result.

## December 2012: BBC announces employment test

The BBC decides it needs its own employment status test.

## April 2013: IR35 office holders exemption removed

IR35 legislation is amended to remove the exemption of office holders. Subsequently, office holders in various organisations, including non-executive directors and interims in financial director roles are forced to apply IR35.

## April 2014: House of Lords PSC enquiry

House of Lords Select Committee on Personal Service Companies publishes report heavily criticising IR35, calling on HMRC to assess the costs and impacts of the legislation.

## April 2014: False Self-Employment legislation

The false self-employment legislation comes into force. Rules say that agencies must deduct income tax and NICs at source if the absence of supervision, direction or control (SDC) of the worker cannot be proved. Despite concerns in contracting circles, HMRC confirms that limited company contractors are excluded from the rules.

## July 2014: BBC reveals employment test

The BBC publishes its one-page questionnaire employment test in response to the media attention to public sector off-payroll arrangements.

The test is proven to be fundamentally flawed, bearing no resemblance to the tests of employment that underpin IR35.

## April 2015: BETs abolished

HMRC announces plans to abolish BETs in October 2014 after contractor clients mistake it for an IR35 status test and they become unworkable. BETs subsequently scrapped in April 2015.

## July 2015: IR35 is highly complex and expensive

OTS publishes analysis confirming that IR35 is both the most complex in its guidance and expensive in terms of compliance for small businesses and HMRC.

## May 2016: Off-payroll working in the public sector

HMRC releases consultation proposing plans to shift the IR35 compliance burden and tax liability in the public sector onto agencies and hirers.

Plans to legislate the changes in April 2017 are later confirmed in the November 2016 Autumn Statement.

## October 2016: HMRC's public sector witch-hunt

ContractorCalculator breaks news of large scale IR35 clampdown by HMRC, targeting more than 100 BBC presenters operating through limited companies.

Several presenters engaged with other broadcasting organisations also believed to be within scope of HMRC investigation.

## December 2016: Draft legislation published

Draft legislation on the public sector reform is published in December, confirming the arrangements for contractors, clients and agencies.